Easy Weaving

Overshot, Velvet,
Shibori, and More

with Supplemental Warps

Deb Essen

SCHIFFER
PUBLISHING

4880 Lower Valley Road · Atglen, PA 19310

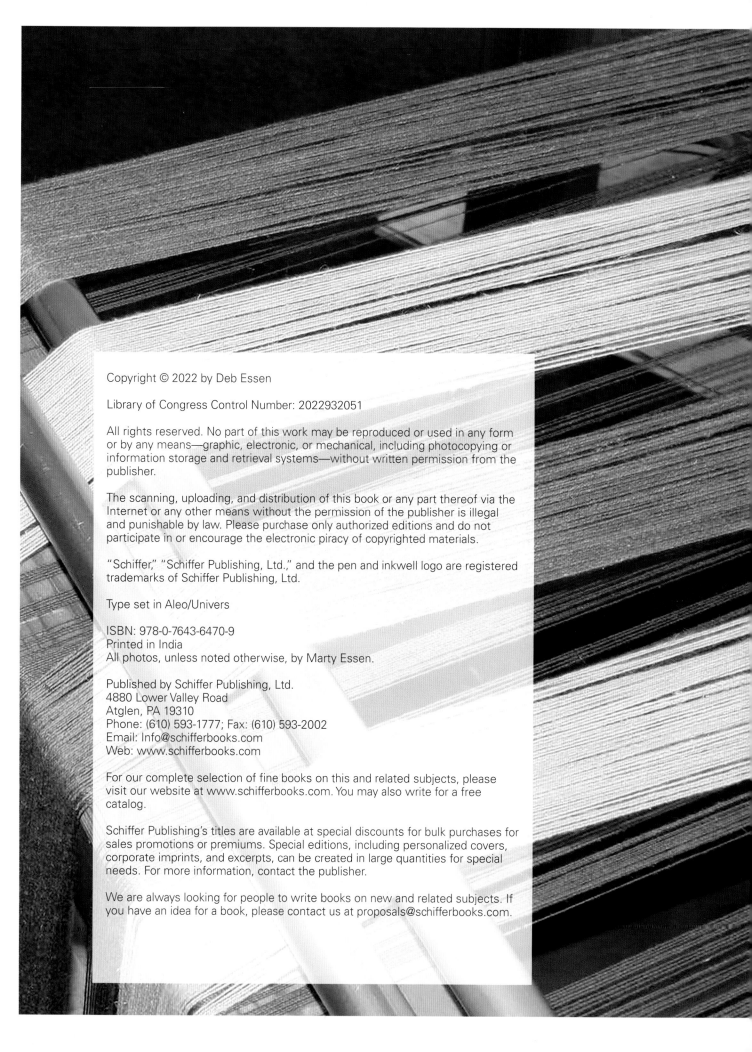

Library of Congress Control Number: 2022932051

Type set in Aleo/Univers

ISBN: 978-0-7643-6470-9
Printed in India
All photos, unless noted otherwise, by Marty Essen.

Published by Schiffer Publishing, Ltd.
4880 Lower Valley Road
Atglen, PA 19310
Phone: (610) 593-1777; Fax: (610) 593-2002
Email: Info@schifferbooks.com
Web: www.schifferbooks.com

For our complete selection of fine books on this and related subjects, please visit our website at www.schifferbooks.com. You may also write for a free catalog.

Schiffer Publishing's titles are available at special discounts for bulk purchases for sales promotions or premiums. Special editions, including personalized covers, corporate imprints, and excerpts, can be created in large quantities for special needs. For more information, contact the publisher.

We are always looking for people to write books on new and related subjects. If you have an idea for a book, please contact us at proposals@schifferbooks.com.

Table of Contents

Introduction

For thousands of years, handweavers clothed both kings and peasants. They wove the sails that made it possible for Christopher Columbus and Magellan to explore the world. They wove humble mattress covers and blankets, as well as exquisite tapestries to warm cold castles and palaces. Their skills were necessary and highly valued.

Then the inventions of the spinning jenny and mechanized looms changed everything. Cloth was woven quickly, readily available, and affordable. Handweaving cloth was no longer a necessity, and it looked like the ancient craft of handweaving would fade away. And it almost did. But the craft has remained alive through the continuing dedication of weavers sharing their skills and knowledge with others.

We are fortunate to live in an age where books are readily available. We have access to a treasure trove of information written down and passed on by generations of weavers. The Internet provides access to blogs, libraries, and information from around the world.

From 2002 to 2004, I undertook a program to complete the Handweavers Guild of America Certificate of Excellence in Handweaving, Level 1. This independent study program requires the completion of 40 woven samples in specified weave structures. The COE program introduced me to supplemental warps. To learn about these weave structures, I had to dig into numerous old books and magazines (thank goodness for guild libraries!) and search on the Internet. As I pieced together information, I often muttered, "It would be really nice if this information were available in one place."

That's when the idea for this book started to perk in my brain.

Over the years I have developed my own methods of working with supplemental warps. My looms don't have a second back beam, but that doesn't stop me. I've learned a lot of lessons the hard way. There was a lot of muttering, fussing, and, yes, cursing, as I worked through my first projects. The first time I wove velvet and had to cut the pile warps on the loom, I broke into a cold sweat. But time, practice, and research have led me on a wonderful adventure in cloth.

This book is not intended to be an in-depth study of all the weave structures using supplemental warps. Rather, it's an introduction to supplemental warp weaves, laying a foundation for your further exploration. You may notice some information briefly repeated in different chapters. This is done on purpose so you do not have to read the entire book from the beginning to explore the different weaves. If you need more information, chapters with more in-depth information are noted.

This book would not be possible without the many weavers who have passed on their experiences and taken the time to write it down. As you explore, I encourage you, too, to write it down so that our craft continues to be enjoyed for generations to come.

May you weave long and prosper.

CHAPTER 1

A New Perspective on Pattern: Creating Supplemental Warp Drafts

A SUPPLEMENTAL WARP IS SIMPLY AN EXTRA WARP that weaves pattern the length of the fabric over a background cloth, much the way a supplemental or "pattern" weft weaves pattern the width of a fabric. You are already familiar with supplemental warp fabrics: the terry-cloth towels in your kitchen and that velvet holiday dress are supplemental warp pile fabrics. Some of the decorator textiles in your home may also be supplemental warp fabrics. Maybe you have a commercially woven table runner with pattern areas that run lengthwise in the fabric.

Supplemental warps have so many possibilities! Instead of being limited to weaving pattern from selvedge to selvedge, you can have stripes of pattern running the length of your fabric, alternating with areas of ground cloth. Supplemental warps can also create 3-dimensional fabric. In this book, there are patterns to create fabric that goes "poof" with Bedford cord and piqué. Supplemental warps can be used to create pile fabrics such as terry-cloth and velvet, and we can use them to create pattern through resist-dyeing techniques—woven shibori! And whereas selvedge-to-selvedge, supplemental weft patterns require at least two shuttles, one for the background weft and one for the pattern weft, supplemental warp patterns require only one shuttle to weave the fabric.

We can change supplemental weft patterns such as overshot into supplemental warp patterns by "turning" the draft. "Turning a draft" is a shorthand way of saying that the threading becomes the treadling, the treadling becomes the threading, and we adjust the tie-up so it works. In a turned draft, supplemental *warps* create the pattern, and the pattern runs lengthwise on the fabric.

Once we turn the drafts, we can isolate pattern sections so they stand out against the plain-weave fabric. My favorite use for supplemental warps is to turn an overshot draft to run lengthwise and break the patterns into sections, letting the designs stand out against the background plain weave.

Computerized weaving programs make turning drafts a breeze. I was never a fan of drawing out designs on graph paper: Coloring in the little squares, erasing, coloring, erasing (ad infinitum, ad nauseum) took some the fun out of weaving design. Then I got my first computerized drafting program! With a click of my mouse, I could turn drafts, change weave structures, colors, tie-ups, treadling, and threading. I was in heaven. I blissfully wove project after project.

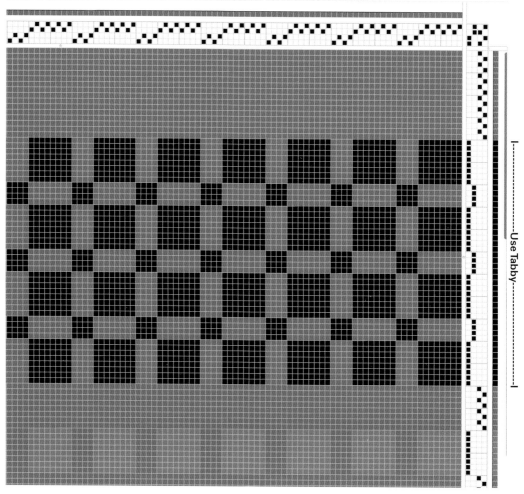

Figure 1. Traditional 4-shaft monk's belt draft

Then, one day, I realized that I didn't fully understand what changes occurred to a draft when I clicked the Turn Draft option on my computer. Now I don't need to know how an engine works to drive a car, but I do need to know what buttons and pedals to push and when to push them! I felt I should also understand the "why, and what happens when" concepts of turning weaving drafts. So I studied what happens to the threading, tie-up, and treadling when the computer turned a draft for overshot. It was worth every minute. It's so much easier to design successful fabrics with turned drafts knowing how it all works.

To help you understand supplemental warp fabrics and what happens when we change a pattern to happen in the warp, let's practice turning drafts for monk's belt and overshot.

Turning a Monk's Belt Draft

Traditional monk's belt is a block-weave structure consisting of a plain-weave background, or "ground" cloth,

and supplemental weft floats that create blocks of pattern across the cloth The cloth is woven by alternating a pick of background weft (also called "tabby") and a pick of pattern weft, so it requires two shuttles. Traditionally, the ground weft is the same weight as the warp yarn (usually the exact same yarn), and the pattern weft is a soft yarn, usually twice the size of the ground warp and weft to ensure that the pattern floats fully cover the plain-weave ground cloth.

The pattern weft in monk's belt floats alternately on the right or wrong side of the ground cloth. You can weave horizontal stripes of just plain weave, but when you weave pattern, the pattern weft must weave from selvedge to selvedge.

Turning the monk's belt draft allows the floats to run the length of the cloth, the pattern areas can alternate with vertical stripes of plain weave, and you can weave pattern using only one shuttle.

This weave structure is deceptively addicting to design

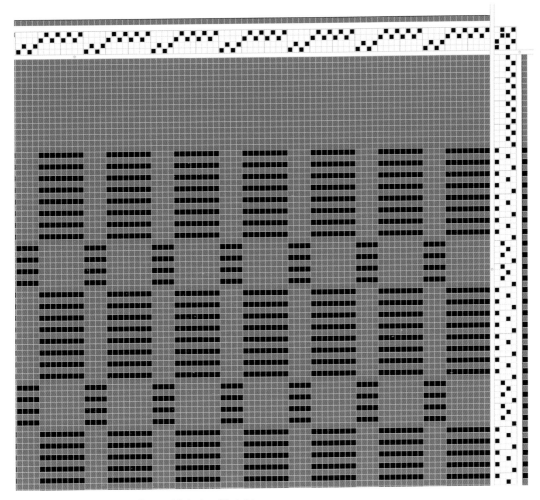

Figure 2. Traditional 4-shaft monk's belt with tabby

with a supplemental warp. You can create almost limitless combinations of colors, block sizes, and spacing between the sections of supplemental warps. All you have to do is turn the draft, so let's get started.

We'll begin by examining a traditional monk's belt draft. **(See Figure 1.)**

Looking at the tie-up, you can see that treadle 3 is tied to shafts 1 and 3 and treadle 4 is tied up to shafts 2 and 4. To weave the plain-weave ground, you would alternate treadles 3 and 4.

To create pattern across the fabric you use treadles 1 and 2. Stepping on treadle 1 raises all the warp threads on shafts 1 and 2, so a pattern pick will float over the blocks threaded on shafts 3 and 4. Stepping on treadle 2, raises shafts 3 and 4, creating floats over blocks threaded on shafts 1 and 2. Everywhere there is a float on the top of the cloth, there will be plain weave showing on the bottom, and vice versa.

Since this draft does not show the treadling for the tabby picks, the drawdown shows only the pattern floats running selvedge to selvedge. It represents fairly accurately what the finished fabric will look like.

You may have noticed that the sections between the pattern blocks appear to be long warp floats. This is because the computer does not automatically fill in the plain-weave picks between the of pattern picks.

Here's what the draft would look like with all the tabby picks inserted. **(See Figure 2.)**

Now you can see that the sections between the pattern floats interlace in plain weave. "Use Tabby" is not only faster to write out than marking the individual treadling for the tabby picks, leaving out the tabby picks also makes it easier to see the pattern in the drawdown and to read the treadling.

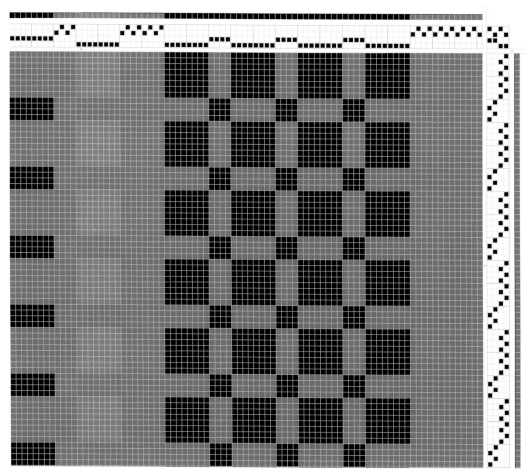

Figure 3. Turned monk's belt with supplemental warp

Now let's turn the draft so the pattern weft becomes a supplemental warp running the length of the cloth. **(See Figure 3.)**

If you look at Figure 3, you'll see that the treadling pattern has now moved to the threading, and the threading has become the treadling. Simple enough, but let's look closer at the tie-up. Notice that it looks nothing like the original tie-up. But turn the draft so that the treadling is at the bottom of the page. Now does the tie-up look familiar? Not only have the treadling and threading changed places, but the tie-up has turned onto its side.

Now look even closer. You will see that shafts 3 and 4 weave plain weave. Every treadle is tied up to one of those two shafts, alternating between shaft 4 and shaft 3 across the tie-up. Shafts 1 and 2 are now the pattern shafts, and one of these shafts is included on each treadle to create floats in the blocks assigned to one of the

two shafts. *The underlying ground cloth and the pattern floats in the supplemental warp are woven simultaneously with every treadle. Only one shuttle is needed, wound with the same yarn as the background warp yarn.*

Here's how the two tie-ups compare side-by-side:

	Traditional Monk's Belt	**Turned Monk's Belt**
Treadle 1	Shafts 1 & 2 Pattern floats over 3 & 4	Shafts 2 & 4 Pattern over Shaft 1 plus tabby over 3
Treadle 2	Shafts 3 & 4 Pattern floats over 1 & 2	Shafts 2 & 3 Pattern over Shaft 1, tabby over 4
Treadle 3	Shafts 1 & 3 Tabby/ plain weave	Shafts 1 & 4 Pattern over Shaft 2, tabby over shaft 3
Treadle 4	Shafts 2 & 4 Tabby/ plain weave	Shafts 1 & 3 Pattern over 2, tabby over shaft 4

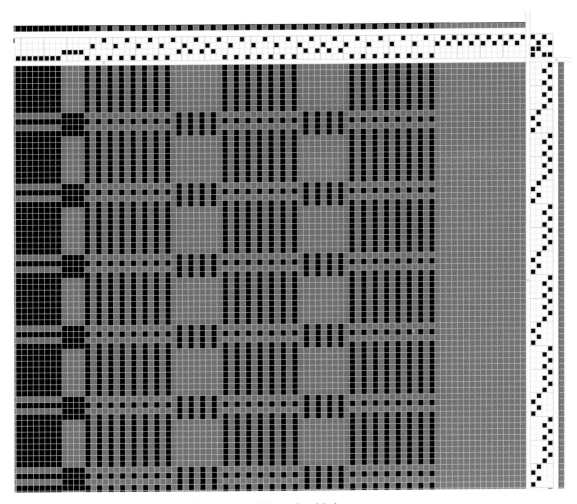

Figure 4. Turned monk's belt draft with background threads added

Again, looking at the draft, there appear to be long floats in the areas between the pattern blocks. Computers are very literal and the program doesn't recognize that the plain weave continues underneath the pattern floats because the threading is not detailed.

Here's how the draft looks with shafts 3 and 4 for plain weave shown threaded as well as the supplemental warp threads on shafts 1 and 2. Now you can see that the plain-weave ground continues across the cloth and is covered in sections by the supplemental warp floats. **(See Figure 4.)**

When I was first learning about supplemental drafts, this was the point where I got a little overwhelmed. I had difficulty following the black and white threading pattern across and checking my threading of background versus supplemental warp threads.

Then I had an idea: I knew treadles 3 and 4 would be threaded in plain weave all the way across the cloth. What if I threaded all of the threads for treadles 3 and 4 across the piece first and then went back to thread the pattern supplemental warp? It works! (Detailed instructions for threading are in Chapter 2.)

Now that you know the plain weave on treadles 3 and 4 continues all across the width of the fabric, you could use a draft like Figure 3, showing just the supplemental warp threading in the pattern sections. Just as the short-

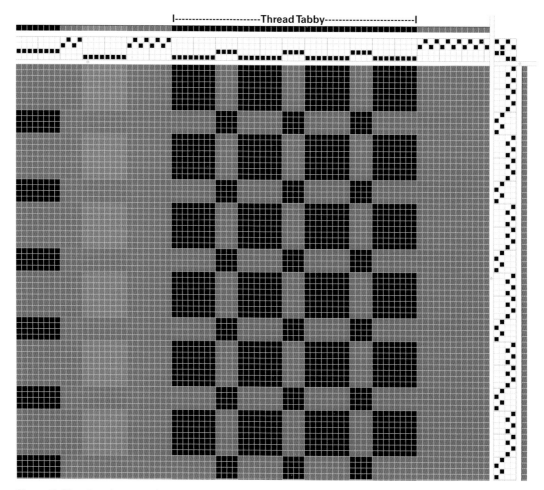

Figure 5. Shorthand way to show supplemental warp with background threads

hand drafts for traditional monk's belt uses the notation "Use Tabby," we could also add a notation "Thread Tabby" above the pattern sections for the supplemental warps. **(See Figure 5.)**

Turning an Overshot Draft

Let's take a look at the steps to turn an overshot draft to make a supplemental warp fabric. Overshot is a twill derivative, which means the overshot tie-up is combina-

tions of the classic twill tie-up of 1-2, 2-3, 3-4 and 1-4. As with monk's belt, floats on the surface of the fabric create pattern. By repeating threading and treadling combinations, these floats stack up to create patterns that are woven with alternating picks of plain-weave ground cloth to create a stable fabric. Unlike monk's belt, overshot has half-tone blocks of pattern where the pattern weft and ground cloth interweave.

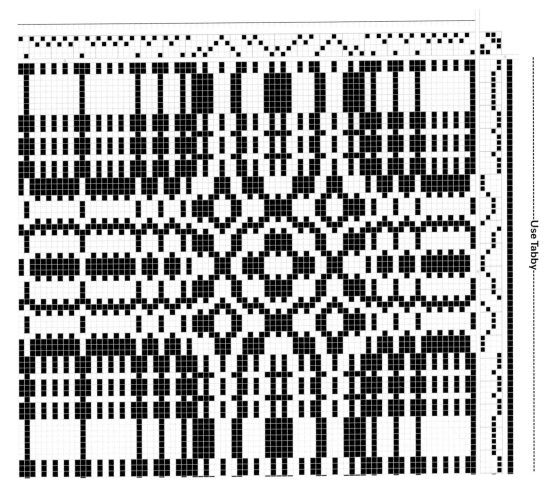

Use Tabby

Figure 6. Traditional 4-shaft overshot draft

ON THE OVERSHOT DRAFTS:
Note My computer program does not show all of the ground cloth interlacements on these drafts. The white warp and wefts are the ground cloth, and where you see what looks like long floats in the white is really plain weave. All of the blue yarns are showing the pattern wefts, running from side to side in the traditional draft and running lengthwise, as supplemental warps, on the turned draft. **(See Figure 6.)**

Figure 6 shows a typical overshot draft. The white threads are tabby and the blue threads are pattern weft. The first four treadles in the tie-up (tied up 1-2, 1-4, 3-4 and 2-3) are for the pattern picks and the last two treadles (tied up for 1-3 and 2-4) are for tabby.

Like monk's belt, to weave overshot, you need two shuttles: one with the pattern weft and one for the ground cloth. When weaving, you alternate one shot of pattern weft (the treadlings marked on the draft) with alternating shots of plain weave (indicated by the phrase "Use Tabby".) Your pattern will cover the entire surface of the cloth from selvedge to selvedge.

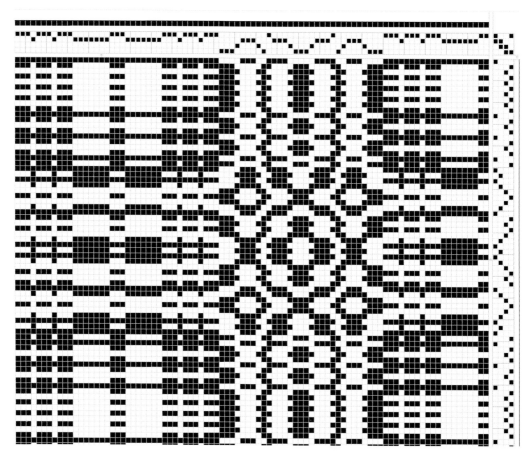

Figure 7. Turned overshot draft

Now let's take a look at the same draft, turned. **(See Figure 7.)**

Comparing the two drafts, the treadling sequence from the first diagram is now across the top of the draft as the threading. The threading sequence from the first diagram now is the treadling. That's pretty easy, just like the monk's belt turned draft.

But look closely at the tie-up. Something's a little different here. You'll note that we now need 6 shafts and only 4 treadles to weave. Shafts 5 and 6 are now the plain-weave (tabby) shafts. Shafts 1-4 are the pattern. But wait! Those pattern shafts aren't tied up the same as in the regular overshot draft. This is key. When turning an overshot draft, you tie up to what were the unraised shafts on the original draft.

To walk through this: To walk through this: in the original draft, treadle 1 is tied up to shafts 1 and 2. On the turned draft, treadle 1 is tied up to shafts 3 and 4 (the open shafts on the original draft). In addition, one plain weave shaft (treadle 6) is included on that treadle.

In the original draft, treadle 2 is tied up to shafts 1 and 4. In the turned draft, treadle 2 is tied to shafts 2 and 3 plus the other plain-weave shaft, 5. Like monk's belt, this enables you to weave ground cloth at the same time as you weave pattern. The pattern is created by the supplemental warps, and you only weave with one shuttle holding the tabby weft.

Here are the tie-ups side by side:

	Original Overshot draft-6 treadles/ 4 shafts	**Turned draft – 4 treadles/ 6 shafts**
Treadle 1	1-2 (pattern) for plain weave	3-4 Pattern plus Shaft 6
Treadle 2	1-4 (pattern) for plain weave	2-3 Pattern plus Shaft 5
Treadle 3	3-4 (pattern) for plain weave	1-2 Pattern plus Shaft 6
Treadle 4	3-4 (pattern) for plain weave	1-4 Pattern plus Shaft 5
Treadle 5	1-3 (plain/tabby weave)	
Treadle 6	2-4 (plain/tabby weave)	

At this point, there's still pattern all the way across the fabric, and you could choose to do that. But we can also choose to break apart the overshot pattern into vertical stripes by inserting sections of plain weave. **(See Figure 8.)**

Note that the ground warp is all threaded on shafts 5 and 6. This is where your computer program comes in really handy— use the Insert key on your keyboard to in-

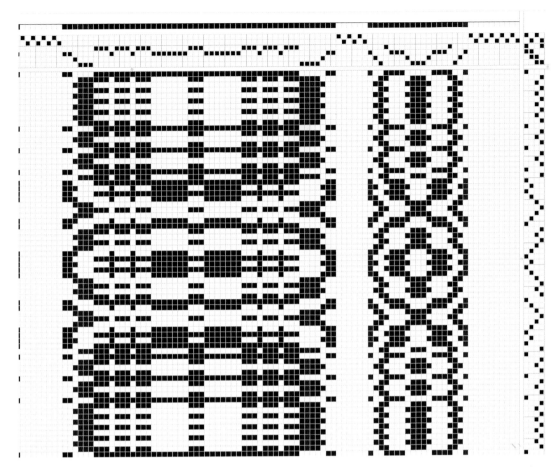

sert the number of threads you want to have in the plain-weave sections, then fill in by alternating threading on shafts 5 and 6.

As with monk's belt, the plain weave continues under the pattern sections to create a stable fabric. Here's what the draft looks like with the plain-weave threading inserted in the first section of pattern. **(See Figure 9.)**

To make threading easier, you can thread all of the background warps on treadles 5 and 6 and then go back and thread the supplemental warps. We'll talk about threading and all the other aspects of supplemental warping in Chapter 2.

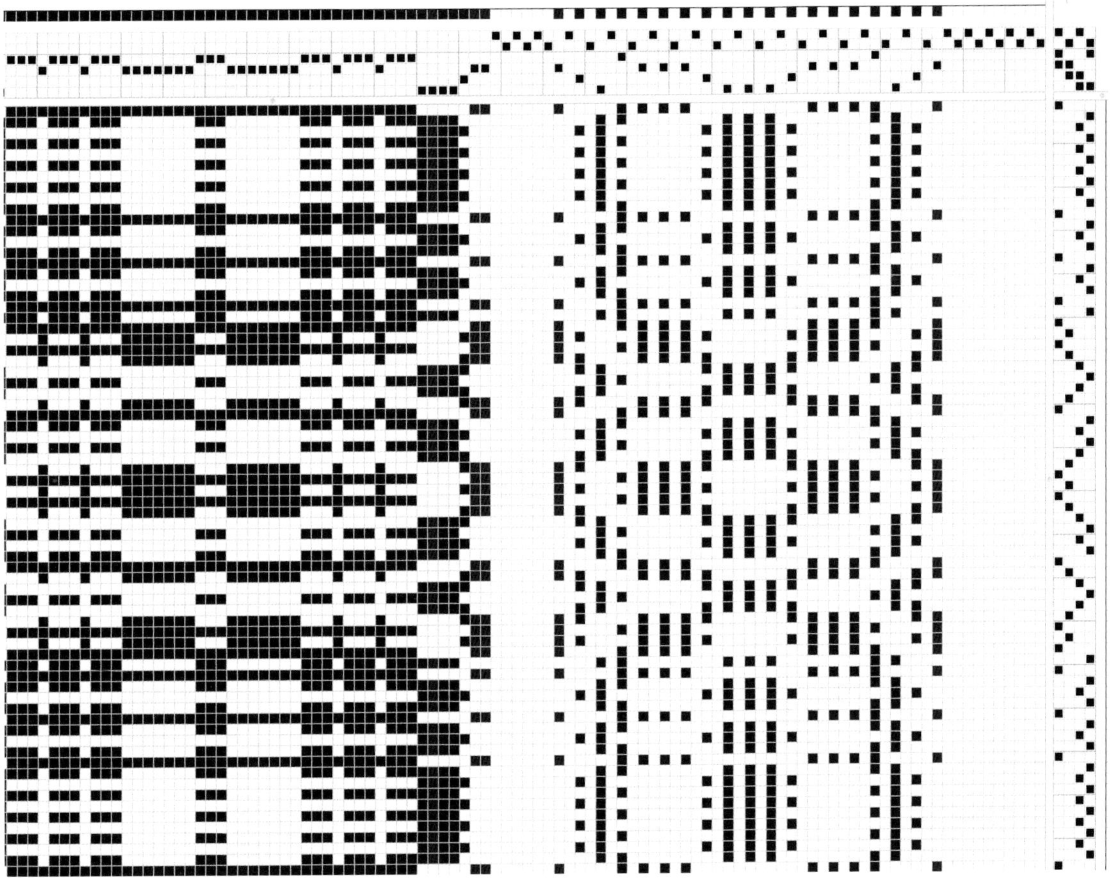

Figure 8. Turned overshot with plain-weave sections added

Figure 9. Overshot draft with ground threads added

Lessons I've Learned About Supplemental Warp Projects.

Now you understand the basics of how supplemental warp fabrics work and how to adapt drafts. In the next chapter, we'll get into the details of warping. But first, here are some lessons I've learned that will make your supplemental warp projects more successful and enjoyable.

Lesson 1: More Yarn is better.

Make sure you have enough yarn *before* you start to wind warps! You can find formulas in the Appendix for calculating background and supplemental warp lengths and amount of yarn needed.

When buying yarn, be sure to check the yards per pound and the cone weight. If your calculations for the amount of yarn needed is really close to the amount of yarn on the cone or in the skein, buy extra. There is nothing worse than running short of yarn because you wound a little looser than intended or ran into knots while winding the warp chain.

if there are different supplemental warp patterns used in different sections, the supplemental warps chains can take up at different rates. (This is especially true for velvet with cut and uncut loops.) If in doubt, add more length to the supplemental warp chains. It's better to have supplemental warp left over than to have a project that is shorter than you planned.

Athena, the Greek Goddess of weaving

For many cultures around the world, the weaving of cloth is very important in both everyday living and mythology. Designs in cloth can symbolize marital status, social status, and tell stories of life and creation.

Athena was a goddess prominent in Greek mythology and one of her roles was the Goddess of Weaving. Being a Goddess, she was, of course, the best weaver! However, a young mortal woman named Arachne was widely known and admired for her beautiful spinning and weaving. Arachne bragged that no one was better than her.

©iStockphoto.com/sedmak

So Athena disguised herself as an old woman and visited Arachne, warning her about being too prideful. Arachne declared she was the best weaver, even better than Athena.

This angered Athena. She revealed herself and challenged Arachne to a weaving contest. Athena wove a picture story cloth depicting her contest with Poseiden. The story cloth was filled with pictures showing the presumptiveness of mortals and the powers of the gods. In contrast, Arachne wove a story cloth depicting the failures and failings of the gods and goddesses.

When Athena saw Arachne's story cloth, she became angry and tore the cloth to pieces. She touched Arachne's forehead causing Arachne to feel guilt and shame. Arachne committed suicide by hanging herself. Athena saw Arachne hanging from the rope and felt pity. Athena changed Arachne into a spider, condemning her and her descendants to hang and weave in dark corners for eternity.

Lesson 2: Know when to walk away from the loom.

On days when everything is going right and I'm "in the zone," weaving is a delight, and woven fabric rolls rapidly onto the cloth beam. However, there are days when nothing goes right and I can feel Athena whispering in my ear to walk away, take a break. Sometimes, she even gives me a small smack on the back of the head to get my attention. When things aren't going right, walk away from the loom. Take a break, relax, and give your "weaver's block" time to work itself out.

Lesson 3: Cut your losses.

Most supplemental warps require only one shuttle to weave, but at some point you will make treadling mistakes and won't notice the error until you are many picks down the line. You have two choices: Let the mistake remain as a "design element" or fix the mistake.

Unfortunately, things can get complicated when you start to unweave. You know what I'm talking about: You start to treadle the pattern in reverse and send the shuttle back through the shed. You catch a warp thread, and the pick doesn't unweave, so you send the shuttle back through the shed and, of course, you catch another warp thread, and then another, and suddenly you have several zigzags of weft tangled across the warp. Grrrrrrrrr!!!

Time to cut your losses, and I don't mean to give up. Rather, I'm referring to an incredibly liberating weaving tip from a class with Madelyn van der Hoogt: Don't use the shuttle when unweaving a mistake. Madelyn instructed us to cut the weft thread at the shuttle. As you treadle in reverse, pull the weft out of each shed from the selvedge edge. Once you get to the mistake, pull out that pick and cut the weft, leaving enough of a tail to fit back into the shed. Press the correct treadle, put the weft tail into the shed, start weaving with the shuttle as like you normally would when changing bobbins, and continue on your way. As Madelyn pointed out, the pennies worth of weft you will be throwing away is much cheaper than the time and frustration you will expend trying to unweave with the shuttle.

Lesson 4: Sample, sample, sample.

Regardless of how many supplemental warp projects I've woven, there are still surprises. Threads don't play well together (too sticky, too thick, too thin, too stretchy), the sett is wrong, colors don't look nearly as good woven together as they did laying side by side in cones or skeins on my work table, there's a threading or treadling mistake in the draft, or I can't get a yarn to tension correctly for love nor money. You want to discover these issues *before* winding long supplemental and background warps.

You can sample using shorter and narrower warps or you can add a foot or so to your project warps for sampling. A separate sample warp is best, and it only needs to be wide enough to include the different pattern threadings and long enough to test the treadling, sett, and yarn issues. Keep in mind, though, that a narrower warp offers less resistance to the beater, so you'll need a lighter beat to achieve your desired picks per inch (ppi).

Adding length to your project warp is next best. About one foot of extra warp will usually gives enough sampling length to work out any issues. At minimum, I highly recommend you add a little length to the supplemental and background warps to work out any problems you may discover once you start weaving.

Lesson 5: Practice makes perfect.

The three most dangerous words in the world are "Can't be done!" The more you practice something, the better you get at it. Your first project will have issues—and that's OK. It's how we learn. Make notes, and correct the issues the next time. Some techniques will feel awkward at first. Is it because the technique is new, or maybe does it need to be adjusted to work better with your loom? Can't wrap your head around the instructions? Follow them step by step at the loom. Before you know it, you'll be an old pro and fabric will flow off your loom.

Lesson 6: Nothing is set in stone.

All of the instructions in this book are based on years of experimenting and weaving with supplemental warps. I've used both jack and countermarch looms, and I don't find one loom style to be superior to the other for supplemental warp weaving. Table looms can be also used for supplemental warp projects just as well as floor looms. You may think of ideas that will work better with your loom, studio, or weaving techniques than mine. If you have an inspiration, try it!

CHAPTER 2

Supplemental Warping in a Nutshell

IN CHAPTER 1, YOU SAW HOW WE MODIFY DRAFTS to make supplemental weft patterning into supplemental warp patterning. But why can't we just beam the supplemental warps together with the background warp? In a nutshell, because supplemental warp ends interlace at a different rate than the background warp threads. Thus, the take-up rate on the supplemental warps is different than the take-up rate for the warp in the ground fabric.

Some supplemental warps, such as the monk's belt we looked at in Chapter 1, weave a pattern via floats on the top and bottom of the background cloth. The pattern warp ends only pass through the background cloth occasionally, as they travel from one side to the other. Because there are fewer interlacements, the supplemental warp takes up less quickly than the ground cloth. Supplemental warps for pile weaves such as terry-cloth and velvet intersect with both the background cloth warp and weft, and the pile loops also take up warp, so they take up faster than the ground cloth. These fabrics need supplemental warp that is two or times longer than the background warp, and we need to be able to easily pull the supplemental warp threads up into the loops needed for the pile.

This difference in take-up rate between supplemental warps and background cloth warps means the supplemental warps cannot be tied to the back apron rod along with the background warp. Supplemental warps need either a second warp beam or a weighting system to keep them in order and under tension for weaving.

But many weavers have assumed they can't weave supplemental warp fabrics because they don't have a second beam on their looms. Well, yes, you can weave supplemental warp fabrics without a second warp beam, and in this chapter, I'll show you how. But first, let's look at some simple and useful tools you'll gather to create your own supplemental warping set-up.

Photo 1. My setup for supplemental warping   **Photo 2. Metal conduit as a tensioning device**

Your Supplemental Warping Toolkit

When we weave any fabric, rule #1 is to keep the warp ends in order. Rule #2 is to maintain an even, proper tension on the warp so that the weft goes in cleanly and can beat in properly. Both of these rules apply for supplemental warp weaving as for any other.

Because supplemental warps and ground fabric warps interlace, and therefore take up, at different rates, supplemental warps need a tensioning system that is independent of the ground-warp tensioning system. To accomplish this, we could wind the supplemental warp on a separate warp beam, but most looms don't come with a second warp beam, and adding one is either impossible due to the loom's construction or, at best, expensive.

Weavers have come up with creative systems to jury-rig a second beam system for supplemental warp weaving. As I was researching this book, I found an article by Rita Buchanan on weaving terry-cloth in *Handwoven* magazine (November/December 2010). She suggested using two looms placed back to back: the first loom for weaving and for holding the ground cloth warp, and the second loom's warp beam to hold the supplemental warp for the terry-cloth pile. While I own a second loom, I don't have enough room in my studio to set my looms up back to back. Fortunately, you don't need to rearrange the furniture or buy another loom to achieve proper tension for supplemental warps.

Here's the bottom line: Humans wove fabrics with supplemental warps for thousands of years before the invention of a second warp beam. I've been weaving supplemental warp fabrics for ten years and don't use a separate supplemental back beam. All you really need are some simple supplies available at your local hard-

ware store plus weights to tension the supplemental warps. It's easy, inexpensive, and accessible to every weaver! So before we get into the nuts and bolts of warping, let's look at the things you'll need.

A Supplemental Back "Beam"

Photo 1 shows my setup for supplemental warp. (That's me in the background, arranging my lease sticks, but more about that later.) You can see the supplemental warp floating above the background warp. It's resting over a temporary back "beam" that I add to my loom when weaving supplemental warp fabrics. This helps satisfy rule #1, keep your warp threads in order. By separating the warps, one will not catch on the other and cause problems as they take up at different rates.

At the front of my loom, the supplemental warp goes through the appropriate heddles for the draft I'm weaving and is sleyed in the reed and tied onto the front apron rod together with the background warp. At the back of the loom, it is held separate from the background warp by a couple of metal pipes sitting on small blocks of wood and held onto the back beam with bungee cords. Easy peasy, and cheap! You can see the pipes resting on the beam. **(See Photo 2.)**

This is aluminum conduit pipe normally used for electrical wiring. However, it works great for tensioning supplemental warps. The pipe comes in many diameters, but a ¾" diameter pipe works best for our purposes. If you ask the hardware store employees nicely, they will usually cut it to the length you want. I recommend cutting it to about the length of your back beam. That will give you lots of freedom in warp width without risking banging yourself on it when you walk around the room.

I have found that conduit pipe works better than large-diameter wooden dowels, as the dowels can develop rough spots, tend to grab the yarn, and can bend under tension. The conduit pipe is very smooth so the supplemental warps move cleanly and the pipe does not bend under tension.

In addition to lengths of conduit pipe, you will need two small pieces of wood to hold the conduit pipe above the back beam, so that the background warp can advance freely, and you'll need two tarp bungee cords like the one shown to secure your tension system at the back of the loom. For the pieces of wood, I use these holders for the heddle on my Beka rigid-heddle loom. But any small pieces of wood will work just as well. **(See Photo 4.)**

Weights, Because Tension is Our Friend

Once you have the two warps separated so that they will remain in good order, it's time to satisfy rule #2: maintaining an even, proper tension for the supplemental warp. Over the years, I've tried many techniques for weighting and tensioning supplemental warps, including sandwiching supplemental warp chains between books stacked on the floor behind my loom. I don't recommend this technique, but it did work. I've used plastic water bottles and half-gallon milk jugs weighted with everything from sand or water to nuts, bolts, washers, and screws. However, these items are bulky, and after a small studio disaster involving a dropped milk jug (the top of which popped off and released water all over the place), I eliminated these items from the warp-weight lineup.

Empty film canisters filled with pennies and/or washers were a favorite for many years. Alas, digital photography has made film canisters hard to find. Prescription pill bottles also work, but the child-resistant caps are frustrating. Small cloth bags with handles or a drawstring, filled with heavy objects, work better than milk jugs. However, if the supplemental warp sections are close together, the bags have a tendency to catch on each other, resulting in uneven tension on the warps. I've also used really big washers hung on opened paperclips. These work pretty well for narrow supplemental warps (and are great for weighting broken warp threads), but there were times when I needed more weight than the number of washers I could stack on the paperclip hook.

Then one day, I was at a friend's house when she had skeins of handspun yarn hanging to dry, and there were weights at the end of each skein.

Deep-water fishing weights! They are perfect! Fishing weights all have a closed loop at one end for attaching to a fishing line, and the loop is perfect for hanging on my paperclip hooks. Fishing weights come in a wide variety of weights from ¼ ounce up to 8 ounces, and they can be found at most sporting goods stores. They are made of lead, so they are compact but very heavy for their size. Because lead isn't good for us, I recommend buying weights that are coated with paint. If you find weights without a coating, you can seal them with a quick coat of spray paint or clear acrylic, so you don't absorb lead through your skin

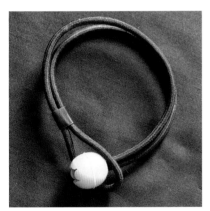

Photo 3. Tarp bungee cords

Photo 4. Heddle holders

Photo 5. Deep-water fishing weights

Photo 6. Kumihimo weights

Photo 7. Angel Wings by Purrington Looms

Photo 8. Hair ties holding threaded warp bundles

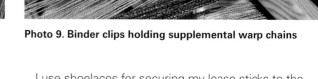
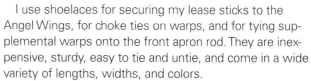

Photo 9. Binder clips holding supplemental warp chains

when handling them.

Another nice option is to use the little weights made for kumihimo braiding. Braiding weights are basically lead fishing weights that come already coated in different colors of plastic. I use these to tweak supplemental warps to proper tension if adding another large weight is too much. I also use these weights when I have to add a single warp thread or replace a broken warp thread.

Regardless what you decide to use, weights are the most important tools in your supplemental warp toolbox.

The Rest of Your Supplemental Warping Toolbox

There are a few other tools that help make supplemental warping easier (and sometimes more fun, if you get creative about it).

The best Christmas present I ever asked for was a set of Angel Wings by Purrington Looms **(see Photo 7)**. They hold my lease sticks for threading back to front. Even if you normally thread front to back, I highly recommend threading your supplemental warps from back to front, because they will be a lot easier to deal with. (More about that when we get into the warping process.)

I use shoelaces for securing my lease sticks to the Angel Wings, for choke ties on warps, and for tying supplemental warps onto the front apron rod. They are inexpensive, sturdy, easy to tie and untie, and come in a wide variety of lengths, widths, and colors.

One of the lessons I've learned over the years is that some of your best weaving tools may not be "weaving" tools. I have many unconventional tools in my supplemental warping toolbox. Hair ties with bobbles on the end are a favorite. I use them in all of my weaving projects, but they are especially handy when working with supplemental warps, where I use them to measure where to start threading the supplemental warp. I take all the background warp threads that won't be in areas with supplemental warps, then I place a hair tie around them in front of the heddles so I can just ignore them while threading my supplemental warp ends. (This technique is also handy for threading block-weave warps. After threading all the heddles for each block, I place a hair tie around the warp threads for that block and push them aside. Then I can see at a glance which block I am threading next. Try it on your next summer and winter or rep weave project.)

Photo 10. A hair pick is helpful when cutting fringe on a rotary mat, but it can also be helpful occasionally to comb out supplemental warps.

Your supplemental warp won't be weighted while you are threading it through the heddles, so it helps to have a way of keeping it neat. You can take the pieces of wood you're using for the tensioning system, lay a wooden dowel or a piece of 1×1 across them on the back beam, and use binder clips to secure the supplemental warp chains to the stick. **(See Photo 9.)**

A hair pick is another unconventional tool I use all the time. I primarily use one at the finishing stage to comb out fringe before trimming. However, if you have a supplemental warp that gets unruly, these picks come in handy to comb out the mess.

Winding the Supplemental Warps

For the background cloth, you can wind your warp as you usually do (although you may find some ideas here that you want to apply to all your warping.) You will wind sets of supplemental warps as individual warp chains that contain the number of warp threads equal to no more than 2" of width in the reed.

For all warp chains, secure the warp cross with a counting thread. The counting thread serves three purposes: it secures the cross, keeps your warp threads in tidy order, makes it easy to insert lease sticks on each

Photo 11. Counting thread in the cross

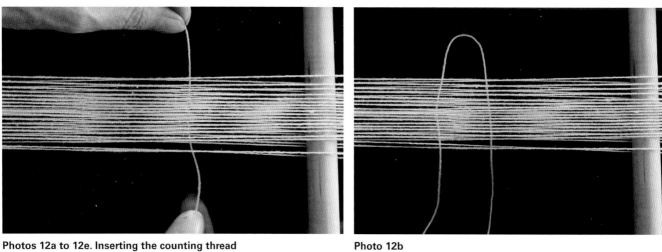

Photos 12a to 12e. Inserting the counting thread

Photo 12b

Photo 12c

Photo 12d

Photo 12e

side of the cross, and bundles together each inch-worth of warps threads **(see Photo 11)**.

If you've never used a counting thread at the warp cross, here's the process: Wind a number of warp ends. Cut a length of contrasting color yarn (or use left-over thrums) that is a least twice as long as the width of your project. I prefer a strong, smooth yarn for the counting thread—5/2 or 8/4 cotton works great.

The "back" of the warp is the first warp thread wound. From the front of your warp, insert one end of the counting thread on one side of the cross between the layers of warp. Bring the end of the counting thread around the back side of the cross and then to the front between the layers of warp **(see Photos 12a and 12b)**.

Count out 1 inch worth of warp threads. Push the counted warp ends toward the back of the warping board and pull the ends of the counting thread into the opening between counted and uncounted warp threads. Overlap the ends of the counting thread so the counted warp threads are trapped in a loop of the counting thread **(see Photo 12c)**.

Count out another inch of warp threads, and push them toward the back. Insert the counting thread ends into the openings on each side of the cross, and again overlap the counting thread ends. Continue until all warp threads are encased in the counting thread. Now you can easily count how many inches of warp you have wound by counting the bundles in the counting thread. Continue warping and counting until you have wound enough warp ends for the project. Tie the counting thread ends in a bowknot **(see Photos 12d and 12e)**.

The counting thread will be removed after you spread the warp in the raddle (back to front threading) or as you sley the reed (front to back warping).

Tie each end of the warp chain and use choke ties along the length of the warp. Insert papers between the layers of the warp on each side of the cross. The inserted papers make easy to divide the warp layers for lease sticks or to insert your hand for threading front to back at the reed. Chain the warp as you remove it from the warping board. **(See Photo 13 and 14.)**

Now wind your supplemental warps. Each supplemental warp chain is going to be at least 10 inches longer than the background cloth warp. This gives you enough warp for the difference in take-up between the supplemental warp and the background warp, and it allows enough supplemental warp length to hang over the back apron rod as you come to the end of your background warp **(see Photo 14)**.

Wind all supplemental warps segments as individual warps, but leave them on the warping board until you've wound all of them. Use individual counting threads on each supplemental warp bout to secure the cross.

Keep your supplemental warp bouts narrow, no wider than 2 inches. Any wider and there will be too much difference between the distance the outer warp threads travel versus the inside warp threads, and you will have tension-

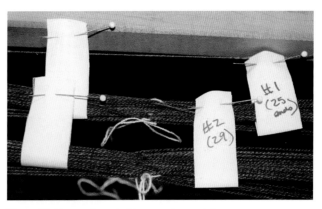
Photo 13. Papers inserted by supplemental warp cross

Photo 14. Using papers to lift warp and insert lease sticks

Photo 15. Weighted supplemental warp hanging over apron rods

TIP: I tie each supplemental warp cross individually and insert papers on each side of the cross of each supplemental warp. Then I number each paper with the order the supplemental warps will be placed on the loom. It may seems like a lot of extra steps, but you only have to lose the cross once or place the wrong supplemental warp in the wrong place, and you will never again begrudge taking a little extra time here.

Photo 16. Choke ties on the warp

ing problems. It is also much more difficult to adequately weight supplemental warps wider than 2" for tensioning.

IMPORTANT: When you tie the choke ties on the individual supplemental warp chains, line the ties up next to each other. This becomes a measuring gauge when you put the warps on the loom **(see Photo 16)**.

Warping the loom

The first time I threaded a project using supplemental warps, I threaded both warps at the same time, and I had difficulty keeping track of which warp thread I should be threading, a background warp thread or a supplemental warp thread. At the time, I was threading a turned overshot draft, and it struck me that all the ground warp ends were threaded on the back shafts, shafts 5 and 6. Hmmmm. Could I thread all of the ground warp threads first on the back shafts and then thread the supplemental warp threads on the front shafts? Eureka! It worked like a charm, and I've used this method for every supplemental warp since.

Turning a draft automatically places the plain-weave background warp threads on the back shafts *if* the plain-weave treadles in the original draft are the treadles on the far right side of the tie-up. To use my threading system with drafts that are already written for supplemental warp weave structures, such as terry-cloth, Bedford cord, piqué, and velvet, you will need to rearrange the threading and tie-up. Chapter 3 will show you easy ways to rearrange these drafts.

Before we dive into the details, here's the basic process for supplemental warping back to front (which I recommend):

- Wind both warps.
- Thread the background warp.
- Thread the supplemental warp.
- Sley both warps together.
- Tie onto the front beam.
- Weight the supplemental warp.

If you choose to warp front to back, you will tie on at the front, sley both warps, then work through the other steps. I'll talk about that at the end of this chapter.

Threading the Background Warp

Thread all of the background cloth warp threads first. For simplicity's sake, all of the drafts in this book use a plain-weave ground cloth. The key to my threading system is to thread the ground cloth warp threads *on the two shafts furthest away from you.*

If you warp from back to front and the draft uses four shafts, then the background warps are threaded on shafts 3 and 4. If the draft uses six shafts, then the background warps are threaded on shafts 5 and 6. As mentioned before, turned drafts will place the plain weave on the back shafts automatically if the original draft has the plain-weave treadles as the far right treadles on the tie-up. For most drafts written for supplemental warps, you will have to flip the drafts to put the background warps on the back shafts. (We'll talk about that in the next chapter.)

> **TIP:** As I am threading the background warp threads, I use a slipknot to tie them into bundles of 4 threads each. Then I can quickly count bundles of warp threads to determine where to start threading the supplemental warps. So, for example, if a project is sett at 10 ends per inch (epi) and the first supplemental warp section is placed 2 inches from the selvedge, 2 inches at 10 epi is 20 warp ends. I can count 5 bundles of 4 warp threads each and use a hair tie (see tools in Chapter 1) to group 5 bundles of 4 warp threads each together. (If you warp front to back, you will be able to count the dents in the reed instead, to determine where to start threading the supplemental warp theads.) **(See Photo 17.)**

Threading the Supplemental Warp Ends

Lay the supplemental warps over the background warps in the proper order for your pattern, with the cross end at the *front* of the loom. Move the cross down the warp chain by pulling evenly on the two layers of the warp chain until you can insert a set of lease sticks. (This is where those papers inserted between the warp layers come in handy.)

Insert the second set of lease sticks on each side of the cross in all of the supplemental warp chains. Secure the supplemental warp lease sticks above the lease sticks for the background warp. Pull the front end of the supplemental warp chains toward the front of the loom until you have enough warp length for threading the heddles. Cut the front end of the warp chain **(see Photo 18)**.

Once the supplemental warp chains are in place, thread the heddles for the supplemental warp according to the draft by pulling the supplemental warp threads one at a time between the heddles that are threaded with the background warps.

The supplemental warp ends aren't attached to an apron rod yet, so it's easy to pull the warp threads forward more than you want. This is when the choke ties we so carefully lined up on the warp chain come in to play. I put a small piece of 1 × 1 on the back beam of my loom, secured in place with my bungee cords, and line the choke ties up across the supplemental warp chains. I use a binder clip to attach each warp chain to the dowel. These clips stay in place until I am finished threading and tied-on to the apron rod. (If you are threading front to back, use the same dowel set up, but on the front beam.) **(See Photo 19.)**

You have the background cloth warp threads counted out already and bundled with a hair tie or piece of scrap yarn, so figure out how far from the selvedge the first set of supplemental warp ends should start, and push all the background threads to that point off to the side.

Take your first supplemental warp thread from the lease sticks (don't undo the cross) and pull it from behind the shafts/heddles forward through the opening between the heddles holding the background warp threads for the edge and the background warp threads for the supplemental warp section. Thread the first supplemental warp thread according to the draft.

Now look at your draft. How many background warp threads are there between supplemental warp threads? If there is only 1, push the heddle holding the next background warp thread plus the heddle threaded with the supplemental warp off to the side by the first bundle of background warp threads. Pull the next supplemental warp thread through the opening in the background warp heddles and thread according to the draft. Move that heddle and the next background warp threaded heddle off to the side by the others. Repeat until you have all of the supplemental warps for that section threaded. **(See Photo 20.)**

Photo 17. Bundled and tied warp threads

Photo 18. Lease sticks inserted and secured

Photo 19. Binder clips holding supplemental warps

Photo 20. Supplemental warp threads pulled between ground warp heddles

Photo 21. Bundles of ground warps

If there is a section of background cloth before the next supplemental warp section, count out the number of background warp threads (already slipknotted together in groups of 4) before the next supplemental warp sections, bundle that group with a hair tie, and push it to the side with the completed supplemental warp threading. Continue threading until all warp threads are threaded in a heddle. **(See Photo 21.)**

Sleying the Reed

When both the background and supplemental warps are threaded, sley according to the background warp sett for your project. (Our example project in this chapter is sett at 10 epi, so it would be sleyed 1 thread/dent in a 10-dent reed.) When you get to the supplemental warp sections, think of the supplemental warp and background warps as two layers of cloth. If the supplemental warp were also sett at 10 epi, you would sley each dent in the supplemental warp sections with one background thread and one supplemental warp thread. If your project were sett at 20 epi in both layers and you were using a 10-dent reed, then you would sley two background warp threads per dent, and in the supplemental warp sections, you would sley 2 background warp threads plus 2 supplemental warp threads in each dent.

> **TIP:** When weaving supplemental warp fabrics, the warp ends need room to move past each other as the shafts are raised and lowered, so it's best to use a reed with wider dents even if you are using a fine background yarn. If the warp threads don't have enough room to move when the shafts are raised and lowered, they will catch on each other and cause pattern errors. So, for example, if your background warp were sett at 24 epi, it would be good to use an 8-dent reed rather than a 12-dent reed. The dents in a 12-dent reed would be too narrow to allow 2 background and 2 supplemental warps to move freely. Using an 8-dent reed and threading 3 background threads and 3 supplement warps in each dent allows more room for the warps to move past each other.

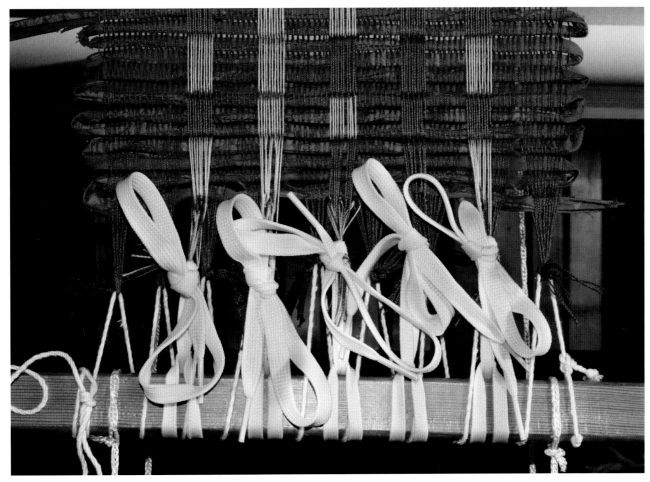

Photo 22. Ground warp tied on with lashing; supplemental warp tied with shoelaces.

Tying on at the Front

I strongly advise using the lashing method to attach your warps to the front apron rod when using supplemental warps. **(See Photo 22.)** It's much easier to get even tension on both background and supplemental warps with the lashing method than it is tying the warps threads directly to the apron rod. The direct tie-on method works, but I've found that it involves a great deal of tying and untying to get all warp threads, especially the supplemental warps, even and well tensioned. (Remember to keep the binder clips on the supplemental warp chains clipped to a stick until you are tied-on and ready to tension the warps.)

Before you begin tying, pull on all warp ends—supplemental and background—until they are the same length and all the slack is out of the warp thread. This is another time where the careful placement of choke ties on the supplemental warps and the binder clips used to temporarily secure the supplemental warps come in handy. Once you have the supplemental warp ends the same length as the background warps, look at the supplemental warp choke ties. Are the choke ties lined up with each other across the warp? They should be. If not, adjust the length of the offending supplemental warp

chain. Once everything is even, clip the supplemental warps to the dowel on the loom beam.

I have two different methods to tie the warp chains to the apron rod using the lashing method.

Method #1: Count 1 inch of background warp threads—include the supplemental warps that are in the same dent as a background warp thread.

So if your project is sett at 10 epi in a 10-dent reed, count 10 *dents* worth of background warps. (If there are supplemental warps in some of those dents, it's still 10 dents worth of warp yarns in the bundles.) Tie all of the warp threads, both background and supplemental, together with an overhand knot. When all warp threads are secured in knotted bundles, lash on to the apron rod and tension the warp. (I'll explain lashing on shortly.)

Method #2: Separate the supplemental warp ends from the background warp ends. (I flip the supplemental warp ends over the top of my beater.) Tie all of the background warp threads in 1-inch bundles with overhand knots. Lash the background warp end bundles to the apron rod. Now go back and tie the supplemental warp ends in bundles 1-inch bundles with overhand knots. Lash the supplemental warp end bundles to the apron rod using the shoelace method.

Photo 23. Ground and supplemental warps tensioned separately

The shoelace tie-on: I love using this tie-on for supplemental warps. I don't have to worry about making the background warp ends and supplemental warp ends the same length, and tensioning adjustments are quick and easy. (Keep the binder clips securing the supplemental warp chains in place through this step.) You'll need one shoelace for each bout of supplemental warp ends. **(See Photo 22.)**

To start, fold a shoelace in half and attach it to the apron rod with a larks-head knot at the point where the warp bout should be tied on. (The warp bout should travel in a straight line from the reed to the apron rod). Use your finger to split the bundle of supplemental warp ends above the overhand knot so you have an even number of warp ends on either side. Holding the warp bout flat, insert both free ends of the shoelace into the

opening from the bottom. Pull on the shoelace ends until you have resistance, then pull both ends down to the underside of the warp threads, cross the ends behind the section of shoelace coming from the apron rod, and bring both shoelace ends back to the top side. Pull on the shoelace ends and tie with a half-hitch knot (the first knot you make when you tie your shoes).

Using a shoelace for each bundle of supplemental warp threads, continue tying the warp chains to the apron rod, tensioning each bundle as you go. Check that the tension feels even and that the choke ties are still lined up across the warps. Make any adjustments necessary. (You can tie each shoelace in a bowknot if you like, but it's not necessary for holding the warp sections securely. However, it does keep those shoelace ends from hanging down and tickling your legs as you work. I've killed many a shoelace end, thinking a bug was crawling on my leg!)

Once you have the warp secured to the apron rods, tie up your treadles and remove the clips from the supplemental warps.

You can get good, even tension with either of these tie-on methods, No matter which one you use, I strongly suggest weaving a few inches with rags or scrap yarn to even out the warp and to help find any tensioning problems or warp-length issues in the supplemental warp sections.

Weighting the Supplemental Warps

Before you weight the supplemental warp, you need to decide how to arrange the two warps on the back beam. **(See Photo 23.)** If the two warps lie together over the back beam, they tend to tangle, especially when the background warp is advanced. When they tangle, the sections of supplemental warp can feed unevenly, causing supplemental warp ends to bubble up or pull too tight in the pattern. To prevent this, I like to weave with my supplemental warps elevated at the back beam above the background warps. If the stick or dowel you used to secure the supplemental warps for threading is smooth and strong enough not to bend under tensioned or weighted warps, you can just remove the binder clips and leave it in place to separate the warps. If it has rough spots that catch the warp threads or bends, re-place it with either a larger diameter dowel or piece of electrical conduit pipe wider than the background warp and secure to the back beam with bungee cords. I actually like to use two pieces of conduit pipe as shown here because they hold the supplemental warp threads nicely in order and they provide a certain degree of tensioning as the threads advance. The pieces of pipe are placed about ½ inch apart on top of small blocks of wood, with the front one under and the back one over the supplemental warp, and then each wood block and the two pipes are secured to the back beam with a bungee cord. **(See Photo 24.)**

Once you have the warps separated, it's time to add weights. The amount of weight you need on each supplemental warp chain will depend on yarn size, elasticity, and the width of the supplemental warp section. You want enough weight on each bout that the supplemental warp weaves smoothly and doesn't bunch up, but not so much that the threads stretch or break. For weights, I recommend using a combination of fishing weights or the kumihimo weights shown earlier in this chapter.

To weight each bout, pull all slack from the supplemental warps and tie an overhand knot at the very end of each supplemental warp chain, leaving a small loop at the very end of the warp chain. This will secure any cut warp ends.

Approximately one foot below the back beam, tie a slipknot in each supplemental warp chain. Place the top

Photo 24. Weighted warps with slipknots hanging at the back of the loom

Photo 25. Warp chain tensioned around a dowel

of a paperclip hook in the slipknot loop. Hang your weight from the bottom of the paperclip hook. As the warp is taken up in the weaving, you will have to untie and re-tie these slipknots until the warp chains are short enough that you can hang the weights at the end of the chains.

There! You are warped and ready to weave!

Warping Front to Back

If you warp from front to back, you will thread your background cloth warp threads on shafts 1 and 2 so that the supplemental warp shafts are closest to you when you thread from the back of the loom. You will have to flip the background and pattern shafts for turned drafts, but the drafts that are originally designed for supplemental warp fabrics will work without making any changes.

The particulars of the warping tasks are mostly the same as for warping from back to front, but you sley the reed first. Sley all the background warps first. Next, sley the supplemental warps in the proper spacing, then lay

the supplemental warp ends across the top of the shafts or castle. Now follow the threading instructions below for pulling the supplemental warp threads through the background warp threads. Next, thread the background threads on shafts 1 and 2, and then follow the instructions above for threading the supplemental warps.

Troubleshooting

Sometimes despite all your efforts and care, you will have problems. Here are some of the most common problems and what to do to solve them.

The supplemental warp threads keep bubbling up and won't lay flat when I beat them into place.

You need more tension on the supplemental warp chains. Put more weight on each chain. If the supplemental warps still bubble up and you've run out of weights, add more tension to the warp chain by taking off the weights, wrapping the supplemental warp chain once around the dowel or metal rod on the back beam, and then replace the weights. **(See Photo 25.)** I often use this method when using knitting yarns for the supplemental warps. Weights alone often don't keep knitting yarns under enough tension to weave cleanly.

Only one or two supplemental warp threads in a section bubble up and won't lay flat.

The bubbling threads are longer than the others in that bundle of warp threads. You need to bring the wild ones in line with the rest of the threads in that section by untying this section from the apron rod, pulling the slack out of the warp threads, and re-tying to the apron rod.

The fell line curves up toward the shafts in some sections

If it's the *background* warp sections, you need to re-tension your warps in those sections. That section of background warp threads is under less tension than the sections around it.

If the bump occurs only in a *supplemental* warp section, you have too much weight on that section of supplemental warp. Lighten up the weight and try again.

It's also possible that the combined sett of your supplemental warp with background warps is too dense or the supplemental warps can't compress enough to fit into the spaces between the background warp threads. If changing the tension and weight doesn't solve the problem, you need to re-examine your supplemental warp yarn selection. One option is to use a smaller supplemental warp yarn. The other option is to change to a more open sett and re-sley the entire piece. You can try re-sleying just the supplemental warp so that there are fewer supplemental warp ends in each dent. If you have two background warp threads and two supplemental warp threads per dent, you could change to one supplemental warp thread per dent. However, this last option can open a whole Pandora's box of problems. Changing the sett of the supplemental will change the width of the supplemental section. Removing extra supplemental warp threads will solve the problem of widening the pattern section but could create gaps in the pattern. Sampling, sampling, sampling up front will save you a lot of headaches later on.

The fell line curves down toward the front beam in some sections.

If the dip is in the *background* warp sections, you need to re-tension your background warps in those sections. That section of warp threads is pulled tighter than the sections around it, thus this section is under higher tension than the sections next to it.

If the dip occurs only in a *supplemental* warp section, you don't have enough weight on that section of supplemental warp. Add more weight and try again.

My selvedges are pulling in a lot—especially on one side.

When you beat the weft into the shed, that weft thread has to travel over and under all of the background warp threads. To allow some extra weft for that up and down travel, you need to make sure you place your weft into the shed at an angle. (This is called "the weaver's angle.") Start by placing the weft at a 30-degree angle in the shed, and adjust from there. If the selvedges are still pulling in, you need more weft: place the weft at a larger angle in the shed. If the weft bubbles out in a little loop at the starting selvedge, use a shallower angle in the shed. (Loops at the selvedge can also be caused by the weft thread not snugging up to the selvedge thread.)

Always beat on a closed shed. This locks in the extra weft thread of the weaver's angle by starting the over/under journey through the warp threads.

My selvedges are uneven and sometimes there are little loops of weft sticking out.

Watch your weaver's angle, and always beat on a closed shed.

Check whether you are throwing the shuttle harder with one hand (usually your dominant hand, the one you use for writing). Throwing the shuttle harder will increase its speed and will pull the weft thread tighter at the selvedges. Those little loops on the edge mean you aren't throwing the shuttle as hard from that direction and the weft isn't snugging up to the selvedge threads.

Also make sure your bobbins are wound firmly and evenly. If the noise from the bobbin stays consistent as you throw the shuttle across, it's wound evenly and feeding smoothly. If you hear a change in pitch (the rattling sound gets louder and faster), the weft is getting caught on itself as it comes off the bobbin, putting tension on the weft as it feeds off and pulling on the selvedge threads.

To prevent pulling, wind the weft onto the bobbin by holding the weft thread between two fingers and pulling back ever so slightly when feeding it onto the bobbin. Cross the weft back and forth at an angle across the bobbin instead of building it up straight like a spool of thread onto the bobbin. This will help the weft feed smoothly off the bobbin. The weft thread on the bobbin should feel firm, not mushy when you squeeze it with your fingers.

If you have one, you can also use an end-feed shuttle. Weft feeds so smoothly off a good end-feed shuttle, they are worth every penny you pay for them, especially when weaving with finer threads.

CHAPTER 3

Flip a Draft the Easy Way

THE EASIEST WAY TO THREAD SUPPLEMENTAL WARPS is to thread the ground cloth warp first, on the shafts furthest from you, and then to thread the supplemental warp on the shafts closest to you. That way, the supplemental warp can be arranged neatly above the ground cloth warp, and it's easy to see and move the heddles you need for the supplemental warp threads.

Sometimes you will have to "flip" a draft to make this possible. "Flipping" is not the same as turning a draft. Turning a draft means switching the threading and treadling. Flipping a draft simply means switching the positions of the supplemental warps and ground cloth warps so the ground cloth warps are threaded on the shafts farthest away from you.

When to Flip

The need to flip a draft depends on two things: the draft itself, and whether you want to thread back to front or front to back. When you turn a draft for a traditional supplementary weft pattern such as overshot or monk's belt, the ground cloth warp ends will be automatically assigned to the back shafts of the loom (the ones closest to the back beam) *if* the ground cloth shafts on the original draft are assigned to the last two treadles in the tie-up. If you plan to warp back to front, you're all set because you will be threading from the front of the loom, so you can thread the ground cloth on the back shafts and be ready to thread the supplemental warp.

If you are threading from front to back, you will be threading from the back pf the loom, so you'll need to flip the draft to put the ground cloth warps on the shafts furthest from you while threading which means the plain-weave ground cloth warps will be on shafts 1 and 2.

Traditional drafts for supplemental warp weaves, such as terry-cloth, velvet, Bedford cord and piqué, assign the supplemental warp threading to the back shafts and the ground cloth on the front shafts (the ones closest to the breast beam). If you warp front to back, you won't need to flip these drafts because the ground cloth warp ends are already on the shafts furthest from you when you're threading from the back of the loom. If you warp back to front, you need to flip the draft so the supplemental warp is on the front shafts and the ground cloth warp is on the back shafts.

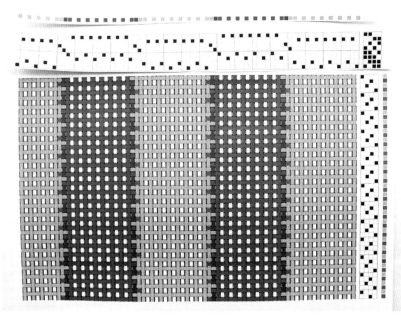

Photo 1. Cut apart the threading, drawdown with treadling, and warp color sections.

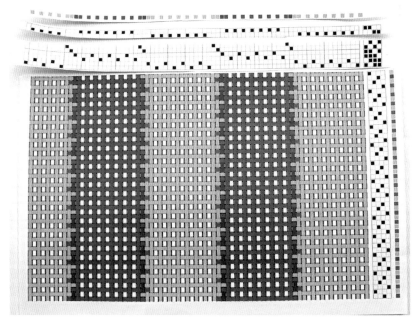

Photo 2. Cut apart tie-up and threading for the supplemental and ground warps.

How to Flip

I've found two really easy ways to flip drafts. One is very low tech; the other is high tech, using your computer drafting program.

The Low-Tech Method

This method is a chance to get out your scissors and glue, and who doesn't love that? First, make a photocopy of the draft you intend to use. The draft in the photo is for traditional Bedford cord, which uses supplemental warps to stuff the plain-weave ribs on the fabric face. The supplemental warps are typically on the back shafts, shafts 7 and 8, with the ground cloth warps on shafts 1–6. This is fine if you plan to thread from front to back, but if you want to thread from back to front, you'll need to flip the draft.

A quick side note about this draft: Up to this point we've talked about supplemental warp projects with a plain-weave ground cloth and pattern supplemental warp. In Bedford cord, supplemental stuffer warps are encased between the plain weave on the top of the cloth and long weft floats on the back to create dimen-

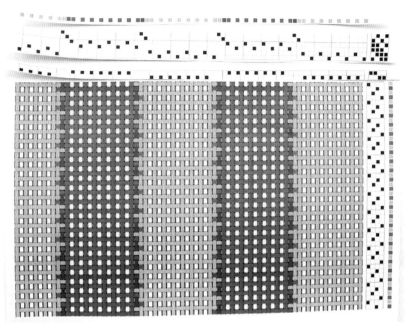

Photo 3. Exchange the ground cloth and supplemental warp sections, putting the warp colors at the top.

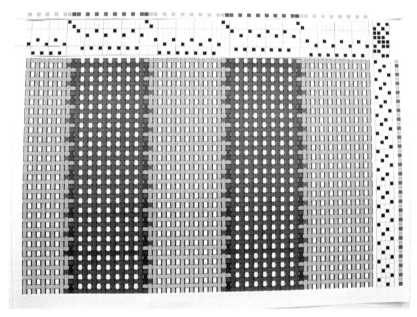

Photo 4. The flipped draft

sional ribs that run the length of the fabric. The draft used in our example is written to show the full drawn-out threading of supplemental stuffers and plain-weave ribs at the same time. (The Bedford cord project chapter shows what a finished project looks like and explains in detail how Bedford cord works as a weave structure.)

To flip this draft, cut across the draft at the very bottom of the threading and tie-up section. Now cut off the very top section showing the warp thread colors **(see Photo 1)**.

On the line between the shafts assigned to the supplemental warps (shafts 7 and 8) and the shafts assigned to the ground cloth ribs (shafts 1-6), cut the draft apart *through both the tie-up and threading*. You now have

three sections: The warp color sequence, the supplemental warp threading and the ground cloth threading including the tie-up assigned to those shafts **(see Photo 2)**.

Trade the positions of the supplemental threading/tie-up section and the ground cloth threading/tie-up, then put the color changes at the top **(see Photo 3)**.

Carefully place the pieces so the tie-up, threading, and warp color sequence all line up again, then tape them together or glue them to another sheet of paper. You now have a flipped draft. You may want to photocopy the draft in its new form and use the photocopy to work from for threading and weaving **(see Photo 4)**.

Screen shot 1. Traditional Bedford cord draft

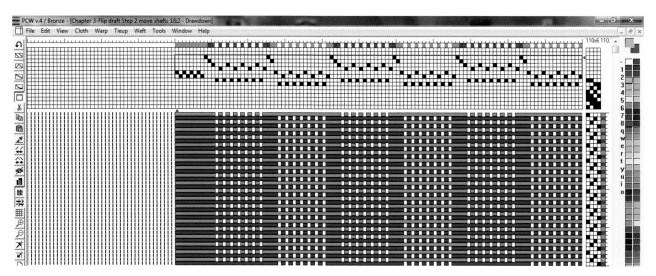

Screen shot 2. After adding shafts, move ground cloth threading above supplemental warp threading.

The High-Tech Method

1. To flip the draft with a computer program, first set your draft to use more shafts. In my drafting program, this command is under Tie-Up. You will need to add as many extra shafts as you are moving for the ground cloth. More is better. You will be getting rid of the extra empty shafts later.

2. Now, you will move the ground-cloth threading using the Cut and Paste functions. Highlight the ground-cloth threading rows, click on Cut, then paste the threading in the blank rows *above* the supplemental warp threading.

3. Now highlight the tie-up section for the shafts that you just moved, cut and paste it in the empty tie-up rows next to the shafts you moved.

4. Next, highlight and cut the <u>entire</u> tie-up section of the draft, and paste it to the bottom of tie-up section.

5. Finally, highlight and cut the entire threading section and paste it to the bottom of the threading, then reset the number of shafts to the original number (in this case, 8). Done! Now you're ready to warp and weave.

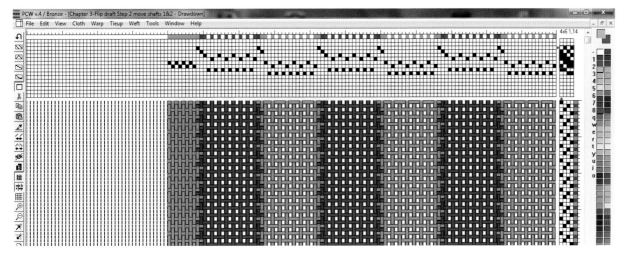

Screen shot 3. Move ground cloth tie-up above supplemental warp tie-up.

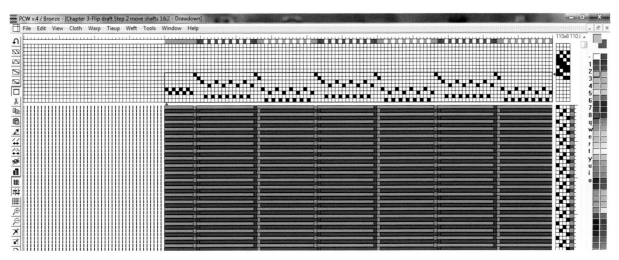

Screen shot 4. Move all threading to front shafts.

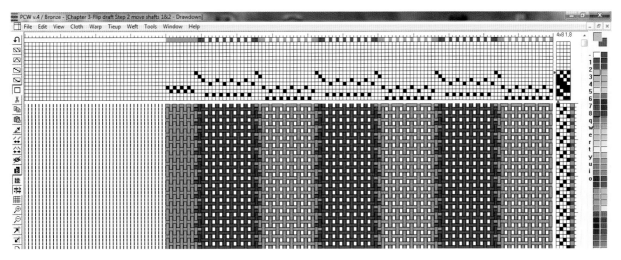

Screen shot 5. Move all tie-up to align with front shafts.

CHAPTER 4

Project Planning

SUPPLEMENTAL WARP FABRICS CONSIST of a background fabric, usually in plain weave, with the supplemental warp providing pattern or texture running the length of the project. There are some special considerations for planning supplemental warp projects.

Selecting the yarns

Selecting yarns for plain-weave ground fabric follows the same rules as selecting the yarns for any regular plain-weave project.

Choosing Yarn

You want a yarn that is strong enough to hold up under tension and take the abrasion of the reed and heddles without breaking. If a yarn breaks easily, it probably isn't a good candidate for a warp yarn. However remember, there is strength in numbers and finer yarns that are easier to break can work fine with support from their neighbors. My test for fine warp yarns is that if the yarn breaks with a good SNAP sound, it is strong enough for warp. If it breaks with a dull "thunk" or with no perceptible sound, save it for weft.

Stretchy yarns, (i.e., most knitting yarns) are a challenge to use for warps. **(See sidebar Weaving with Knitting Yarns)** I suggest steering away from stretchy yarns for the background fabric, but they can work well for a supplemental warp. I wove a favorite scarf using bamboo weaving yarn for the background cloth and bamboo sock yarn for the supplemental warp.

Avoid hairy yarns such as mohair or any novelty yarn, such as eyelash yarn, that has long strands sticking out. You would not believe what a snarled mess they can create, even as weft.

Last, but not least: The loftier the yarn used for the supplemental warp sections, the greater the size difference you can have between the supplemental warp and background warp threads. Lofty yarns compress well because there is more air in the yarn, so even a yarn over twice the size of the background yarn can work. However, a tightly spun yarn like a 5/2 pearl cotton will be very hard to beat into a 10/2 background warp, because it can't compress enough to pass through the spaces in the background cloth without distorting the fell line. Think of squeezing the middle of a down pillow. There's a lot of air within the down and it's easy to create an hourglass shape. However, a pillow stuffed with springy polyester batting cannot be compressed into the same shape. Sampling with the supplemental warp yarns is really, really important.

Weaving with Knitting Yarns

Yes, you can weave with knitting yarns —as long as you don't expect them to behave like weaving yarns. By working with, rather than against, knitting yarns' characteristics, great things can happen.

Most knitting yarns are spun so the yarn has more loft (air) and elasticity (spring) than weaving yarns. This can range from very little loft and elasticity (many lace weight yarns) to the fiber equivalent of a rubber band (wool crepe). Knitting yarns can make wonderful supplemental warps: So many colors, textures, and highlights are available, and why should knitters have all the fun?

Most knitting yarns are *woolen-spun*, meaning that the fiber is carded into roving and spun so that air is incorporated, creating loft and elasticity in the yarn. Most weaving yarns are *worsted-spun*: The fibers are combed to lie in the same direction and spun in the same direction as the aligned fibers, so the fibers pack tightly together. Denser fibers mean less elasticity in the yarn.

When you use knitting yarns in a warp or supplemental warp, you have to plan for the elasticity in the yarn. Take-up is going to be much greater than a weaving yarn because the knitting yarns stretch so much under tension and then return to their original size when removed from the loom. I've woven projects out of wool crepe knitting yarns that shrank over 7 inches when I took them off the loom. You may need to add a tensioning device in addition to weights on the supplemental warps to keep the yarns under enough tension while weaving. Sample your yarn choices before committing to a full project to learn what adjustments you may need to make.

Knitting yarns have a different sizing system than weaving yarns. In this system, thickness is referred to as "weight," even though it has nothing to do with weight. From finest to thickest, the knitting yarn sizes are:

superfine (laceweight)			plain-weave sett
	wpi	yd/lb	
wool	30–40	5,000–6,000	18–28
cotton	25–68	2,000–8,000	15–40
linen	28–54	2,100–4,200	14–30
silk	30–100	2,800–17,000	15–65
bamboo, Tencel, etc.	30–84	3,360–12,600	15–48
fine (fingering or sportweght)			
wool	14–22	1,500–2,800	8–14
cotton	15–24	1,000–2,000	8–12
sock	18–20	about 2,000	8–15
silk	14–22	1,100–2,000	8–12
DK (double knitting)			
wool	11–16	900–1,500	6–8
blends	15–16	1,000–1,250	8–10
silk	14	1,500	8–10
bamboo, Tencel, etc.	12–22	1,000	10–12
medium (worsted)			
wool	10–12	640–1,000	6–8
wl/blends	10–13	800–1,200	4–8
cotton	10–13	630–900	5–8
cot blends	12–16	840–1,000	7–9
alpaca, angora blends, etc.	12–18	1,200–2,200	6–8
bulky			
wool	6–10	250	4–6
wl/blends	6–10	280–800	4–6
alpaca	7–8	490–600	4–6
super bulky			
wool and wl/blends	4–7	260–420	4

And just to keep things interesting, in these designations, the term "worsted weight yarn" also has nothing to do with how the yarn was spun. The yards/lb and setts for each of these weights varies, depending on the fiber. There's a lot of variation, and you really need to do the wraps-per-inch test and sample, but there is a yarn guide at the Weaving Today web site that you can use to get started. (Look under Tools and Resources/Weaving Supplies at www.weavingtoday.com.)

Note on Bradford Count

When I took my first weaving class, yarn sizes made absolutely no sense to me. Why was a 20/2 yarn smaller than a 10/2 yarn, when clearly 20 is a larger number than 10? When I asked my teacher, she told me that it's just something that I'd remember as a weaver. It wasn't until years later when I was reading *In Sheep's Clothing*, by Nola and Jane Fournier, that I learned about the Bradford count and what those numbers mean.

The size of weaving yarns was established by the worsted spinning industry in Bradford, England, to standardize yarn sizes for mechanized spinning and weaving. The Bradford count is the number of 560-yard skeins of singles yarn that can be spun out of one pound of combed fiber. The smaller the spun singles, the more yarn yardage can be spun from a pound of the fiber.

In the United States, the first number in "20/2" is the

Bradford count: twenty 560-yard skeins of singles were spun out of one pound of fiber. The second number is the number of single yarns plied together to make the yarn. European yarns usually reverse these numbers so that the first number is the plies and the second number is the Bradford count.

The Bradford count system was developed for worsted wool spinning, but it has been adopted for other fibers, which is where things get complicated. A 20/2 silk weaving yarn has a larger diameter than 20/2 cotton, and an 8/2 cotton is larger in diameter than an 8/2 Tencel yarn. Therefore, yarns that have the same size designation can have different setts in weaving. So consider the Bradford count as a starting point, and always determine your sett by measuring the wraps per inch divided by 2.

Calculating Sett

Calculate your sett (ends per inch or epi) by wrapping the warp thread around a sett gauge or ruler for 1 inch, making sure you don't pull the threads tight (stretching makes them thinner), and that they lie next to each other without crowding or space between the threads. Count the number of wraps in 1 inch and divide by 2 to get the plain weave sett for the yarn.

Never blindly follow sett charts or suggested setts from the yarn manufacturer. Always calculate your sett. Yarn sizes can vary between manufacturers and will vary with fiber content. An 8/2 Tencel does not have the same sett as an 8/2 cotton **(see sidebar Note on Bradford Count)**.

Calculating Amounts for the Ground Warp

It's relatively easy to calculate background warp amounts. First, calculate the sett for your yarn. For our example, we are going to use 10 epi. We want our finished project to be 8" wide off the loom and after washing, so we need to add an allowance for draw-in. (Draw-in is the amount the project will narrow from side to side after the warp and weft adjust to the over/under weaving sequence.) In general, 10% is a good general allowance for draw-in. So the target width in the reed is the finished width of the project × 1.10. For our example project:

8" finished width × 1.10 = 8.80 inches, so we round up to a 9" width in reed

To calculate the total number of warp ends for the project, you multiply the target width in reed by the sett (ends per inch) For our example:

9" width in reed × 10 ends per inch = 90 warp ends for the background cloth.

Now to calculate the length of each background warp thread, we can also add a 10% allowance for take-up. Each warp thread needs to be the finished woven length plus:

- 10% for take-up
- As much length as you want for sampling
- Allowance for fringe and for loom waste. (The waste amount will depend on your loom. Thirty inches is a good, safe allowance for most looms, and unless you're planning a very long fringe, the fringe can come from the loom waste.)

For our example:

Finished woven length = 65"

10% for take up = 6.5" (round up to 7")

Fringe/header = 5"

Thrum Waste (the warp on the loom you cannot weave) = 18"

65" + 7" + 5" + 18" = 95" warp length

To calculate the total amount of background warp yarn needed for project, just multiply the warp length by the number of warp threads then divide by 36 to get the number of yards needed. For our project,

(95" × 90 warp ends) divided by 36" = 237.5 yards (We can round up to 238 yards.)

Calculating Supplemental Warp Amounts

For most turned drafts (turned versions of drafts that use supplemental wefts), the supplemental warp will be the same length as the background warp chain plus 10–12 inches. (Supplemental warps for weaves such as terry-cloth or velvet are calculated differently, and those calculations will be discussed in the terry-cloth and velvet project chapters.)

Generally, your supplemental warps will be wound at the same sett (ends per inch) as the background warp, regardless of the size of the supplemental warp threads. We will discuss this further in the terry-cloth and velvet project chapters.

> **Note** Computer weaving programs don't understand that supplemental warps float above and below the ground cloth, so their project specifications will add the supplemental warp threads into the total number of warp ends and calculate the width accordingly. In real life, the supplemental warp ends in the threading draft do not add width to your cloth. So computer-generated drafts are perfectly good at showing where to place the supplemental warp threads in relationship to the background cloth warp threads, *but they're not useful for calculating warp amounts for supplemental warp projects.*

Supplemental Warp Striped Scarf Project

THIS SCARF IS A COMBINATION of a plain-weave background with warp-faced stripes based on monk's belt, which is a close relative to overshot. Like overshot, monk's belt is a block weave that creates pattern from selvedge to selvedge using floats of pattern weft over a plain-weave ground cloth. Unlike overshot, in monk's belt there are no areas where the pattern weft interlaces with the ground cloth to create areas of half-tone, You need a minimum of four shafts to weave traditional monk's belt—two shafts for the plain-weave background and two shafts to weave pattern. To add more pattern blocks, you add more pattern shafts in sets of two. The same rules apply to supplemental warp monk's belt.

With traditional monk's belt, you can use different weft colors to weave different pattern blocks, but because the pattern runs selvedge to selvedge, you can't mix two colors in the same block. But with supplemental monk's belt, we can combine two colors in the same supplemental warp chain and get two color blocks in the same threading block. Advantage goes to supplemental warp monk's belt!

I designed this scarf in the winter of 2014. It snowed for days and days and days, and I needed color! I pulled out all of my 10/2 pearl cotton and started combining colors. The brightest colors won.

The sett in the stripe sections is very dense. There are 20 supplemental warp ends and 10 background warps in each stripe. The supplemental warp threads show as floats on the back and front of the fabric in sets of 10 threads on each side.

To achieve the color changes in the stripes, you wind supplemental warps in two colors and alternate threading yellow yarn and pink yarn. This creates squares of color along the stripes where the top and bottom supplemental warp yarns change sides of the fabric.

Here are some warping and weaving tips for this project:

- To wind the supplemental yarn warp chains, wind both yarn colors at the same time, placing a finger between the two yarns to keep them from twisting around each other as you wind. The two colors will not come off the lease sticks in the proper threading order according to the draft, but just move the correct color over as you thread. This tiny movement will not affect your warp tension.

- When the supplemental warp colors switch sides of the ground cloth, sometimes the line between the squares of pattern are not straight because the supplemental warp threads stick together. To unstick them, change treadles, keeping the new shed open, and beat on the open shed. This usually gets all the supplemental warp threads to pop to their new positions. If some still stick, open the shed and run your finger (with some pressure) along the fell line. If you still have problems with clean transitions, you can move the stuck supplemental warp ends by slipping a pickup stick between the supplemental warp ends and the background layer and turning the pickup stick on edge. You should do this on both top and bottom layers.

STEP BY STEP INSTRUCTIONS

Step 1   Wind 174 warp threads 3 yd long of the background warp. Wind 5 separate supplemental warp bouts of 20 threads each, 3 yd long. Wind 3 of these bouts with 10 threads each of pink and yellow, winding the colors at the same time and holding a finger between them to keep the threads from twisting. Wind two more bouts, one with 20 ends of yellow and one with 20 ends of pink. Set the supplemental warp bouts aside. Thread the background warps according to the directions in Chapter 2, following the draft in Figure 1.

Step 2   Lay supplemental warps on the loom as described in Chapter 2. Thread the supplemental warps on shafts 1 and 2 following the draft for colors. Note that the draft shows the background warps in the first stripe only. Each of the remaining stripe sections are to be threaded with 1

Project at a Glance: Supplemental Warped Striped Scarf

STRUCTURE
Plain weave with supplemental warp stripes.

EQUIPMENT
4-shaft loom, 9" weaving width; 10-dent reed; 1 shuttle with bobbin.

YARNS
Background warp: 10/2 pearl cotton (4,200 yd/lb), purple, 522 yd.
Supplemental warp: 10/2 pearl cotton, yellow and pink, 150 yd each.
Weft: 10/2 pearl cotton, purple, 360 yd.

(I used WEBS Valley Cotton Line: # 6277 Deep Periwinkle, #1325 Daffodil, and #6186 Azalea.)

WARP LENGTH
Background warp: 174 ends 3 yd (allows 7" for take-up, 33" for loom waste; loom waste includes fringe). **Supplemental warp:** 100 ends (5 sections of 20 ends each) 3 yd long.

SETTS
Warp: 20 epi (2/dent in a 10-dent reed). In supplemental warp sections, sley 2 background warps plus 4 supplemental warp ends per dent.
Weft: 20 ppi.

DIMENSIONS
Width in the reed: 87/10".
Woven length (measured under tension on the loom): 67½".
Finished size after washing: 7½" x 61½". " plus 5" fringe at each end.

Figure 1. Draft

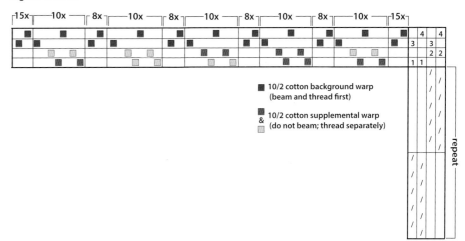

10/2 cotton background warp (beam and thread first)

10/2 cotton supplemental warp (do not beam; thread separately)

background warp between every 2 supplemental warps. Space the supplemental warps across the background warp as follows:

Step 3 Start the first supplemental warp 30 background warp ends from the edge. Bundle the background warp threads and push to the side. Thread the first supplemental warp chain according to the draft, with 1 background warp thread between every 2 supplemental warp yarns including 1 background warp after the last set of two supplemental warps. There should be a total of 10 background warps and 20 supplemental warps in each stripe section.

Step 4 Count out 16 background warps for space between stripes. Bundle and push to the side. Thread the second warp chain with 1 background warp thread between every 2 supplemental warp threads. Bundle and push to side.

Step 5 Count 16 background warps, bundle and push to the side, then threat the third supplemental warp chain. Repeat for the fourth and fifth chains. When you finish, there should be 30 background warp threads left for background cloth to selvedge

Step 6 Sley the reed, centering for a 87/10" weaving width. There will be 2 ends/dent in the background-only areas. The supplemental warp sections will have 2 background warp ends and 4 supplemental warp ends per dent. The supplemental warp stripes will be ½" wide.

Step 7 Tie on using your preferred method, including the pattern warps with the background warp in the tie-on groups. Weight the supplemental warp bouts over the back beam. Adjust your background warp tension to match that provided by the weights. (Add weight if you like to weave with more tension).

Step 8 Wind a bobbin of weft yarn. Leaving at least 5" for fringe, weave the scarf according to Figure 1, moving the weights on the supplemental warp as needed.

Step 9 Cut scarf off loom, allowing 5" for fringe, the tie fringe in overhand knots of 4 background warp threads/knot. In supplemental warp sections, tie knots with 4 background warps plus 8 supplemental warps per knot.

Step 10 Handwash in warm water, lay flat to dry.

Monk's Belt Table Runner

TRADITIONAL MONK'S BELT HAS BLOCKS of design running from selvedge to selvedge. A minimum of 4 shafts is needed—two for the plain-weave ground cloth and two for the pattern—and it is woven with at least two shuttles, one for the ground weft and one for the pattern weft. Threading the pattern blocks in various widths and weaving more or fewer picks of pattern weft results in different patterns across the cloth.

Turning the monk's belt draft makes the pattern blocks run length-wise within a piece. We can thread vertical stripes of any combination of blocks that we like, and we have the option of having sections of plain weave between the pattern stripes and even within the stripe. This is different than what we set up for the striped scarf project in the previous chapter. In that project, we set up the supplemental warps to weave on both sides of the fabric in the same block. The change in colors within a stripe was achieved by winding two colors in that supplemental warp section. The supplemental warps switch between the front and the back of the fabric based on tie-up and treadling. The solid stripes are supplemental warps of the same color threads set to weave on both sides at the same time creating a solid stripe, even when the warps move from front to back and then back to front.

In this table-runner project, the supplemental warp threads move from one side of the fabric to the other, depending on the treadling and tie-up. When the supplemental warp shows on the top, the back side is plain-weave ground cloth and vice versa. (For a more in-depth discussion on monk's belt and how to turn a monk's belt draft, see Chapter 1.)

This project was so much fun to draft. Exploring options with color changes, spacing of the blocks, and changing the size of the blocks occupied me for hours (literally). I wanted to weave a table runner in linen. For years I had had an aversion to weaving with linen. I'd read too many articles about how difficult it is to weave with linen and the need to keep the warp and weft threads wet while weaving. It sounded too complicated and messy! Then I started in the Handweavers Guild of America Certificate of Excellence program, and I was required to weave a sample in linen.

Here's what I learned—linen is not hard to weave with. It just has some unique properties, and you have to understand and work with them instead of against them.

Linen is a *bast* yarn, meaning that it is spun from the long fibers in the stems of a plant; in this case, a flax plant. The flax stems are retted (literally, rotted by exposure to moisture) to remove the outside flesh of the stem and expose the long fibers inside. Those fibers are then beaten to break them apart and *scutched* to scrape away the remaining cuticle and other unwanted bits until you have just the beautiful clean fiber for spinning into yarn. Finally, the fibers are combed through a hackle (a piece of board with nasty-looking, sharp steel points sticking up) to remove all the shorter fibers and any remaining unwanted cuticle. The bundle of long fibers left from the hackling process is called a *strick* of linen, and the shorter flax fibers are called *tow linen.* The long flax fibers are spun into *line linen.* These yarns are smooth, strong, and very inelastic. Even very fine line linen yarn from the long flax fibers has a high tensile strength. Line linen makes wonderful fabric for clothing, towels, and other household textiles. To spin flax fiber into linen yarn, the fiber is dampened with water, which softens the fibers so they will twist together—thus the term "wet-spun" linen.

The shorter tow fibers left from the hackling process are spun into tow linen yarn that is generally coarser than line linen yarns. Because it is made from shorter fibers, tow linen yarn is hairier than line linen, and more likely to shed bits of fiber. On the plus side, tow linen still has very good tensile strength and has a tiny bit more elasticity than line linen. Tow linen yarns make fantastic warps for rugs.

Cottolin yarn is a blend of cotton and tow linen. Depending on who you talk to, cottolin is either a yarn exhibiting the best of both fibers or the worst of both fibers. Personally, I think it can go either way, depending on the yarn manufacturer and how you are using the yarn in a project.

For this project, I used line linen. In my stash, I found some lovely deep-green wet-spun Irish line linen, purchased from Webs once upon a time, and some black and gold line linen by Bockens. (The project specifications have information for purchasing deep green line linen by Bockens that is very close to the same color I used.)

TIPS FOR WORKING WITH LINEN

All line linen is sold on spools rather than cones. Spools do not have a wide base to sit on for winding the warp. I've found several ways to corral these spools during warping without investing in seldom-used equipment such as spool holders or racks.

- Computer CDs are sold on a spindle that holds them in a stack. Empty CD spindles make excellent holders for yarn spools while winding a warp.
- Drop your spool of yarn in a small-diameter can: A 1-lb coffee can works great. The can will corral the spool as the yarn unwinds. It's noisy, but works.
- If you are a handspinner, place the spool of yarn on your lazy kate.
- Poke a wooden dowel through two ends of a shoebox. Insert the dowel through the spool and suspend in the shoebox. Putting a little weight in the shoebox helps to keep box from moving around when winding the warp.

Because of the inelastic nature of the yarn, the linen coming off the spool will want to curl back into the shape it was on the spool, and this can cause you prob-

lems while warping. This curling becomes more extreme the closer to the center of the spool you get. Winding the yarn onto the warping board straightens the yarns, but as soon as you remove the warp from the warping board, the yarn springs back into the curls. To help the yarn relax and straighten, once you have your warp wound, leave it on the warping board, spritz the entire warp chain with water, then walk away and let it air dry. Once dry, the yarn will be straight and you can chain the warp without any trouble. Don't rush the drying process with a hair dryer. I found the heat makes the yarn stiffer and a bit more difficult to work with than if you just let it air dry.

You do not have to wet your weft yarns nor soak the bobbins to weave linen. Wind your bobbins firmly, and move back and forth across the bobbin at a slight angle while winding rather than feeding the yarn straight on like a spool of thread. The yarn will feed smoother off the bobbin this way. If you use an end-feed shuttle, wind the pirns as you normally would, keeping firm tension on the yarn, and building up yarn on the pirn in small increments. Some weavers warn that it's difficult to get tidy selvedges with the linen weft unless the linen is wet, however, I've found the finer linen yarns in this project bend smoothly around your selvedges. You also do not have keep wetting the warp as you go. I live in a very dry climate in Montana, and I don't find I have to wet the warp when weaving, but you could always weave with a humidifier in the room if you're worried about it.

The inelasticity and strength of linen means you can have really taut tension on your ground warp, however, it's more difficult to beat in the linen weft when warp tension is piano-wire taut. Cotton, wool, and other fibers have a little elasticity that lets the warp and weft stretch over and under each other even when they are under fairly high tension, but linen needs a little help to allow for take-up and draw-in. To tension linen, advance the warp until it's taut, then back off the tension just a little: One or two teeth on the pawl is usually enough. This gives the warp room to move over and under the weft. If you live in a humid environment, the linen will also absorb some moisture from the air, which will make it a bit more pliable.

In addition to weighting your supplemental warp chains, you may need to further tension your supplemental warps by either wrapping the warp chains around a dowel before hanging weights on them or by creating another tensioning system to run the warp yarns through prior to adding the weights. (See Chapter 2.)

A firm, consistent beat is extremely important with when weaving with linen. Due to the inelasticity of the linen yarn, it's actually easier to underbeat than to overbeat. Watch your weaver's angle and keep draw-in at the selvedges to a minimum. Linen selvedge threads won't stretch far before snapping. A temple is very helpful for weaving with linen, but remember to move it frequently.

To finish your piece, handwash in very warm soapy water with some agitation, then rinse in warm water. You can either lay the piece flat or toss it into the dryer until it's almost dry. Press the damp fabric firmly with your iron set on the linen or high heat and steam settings. This helps flatten the linen yarns and brings the cloth up to a nice sheen. If the piece gets completely dry before ironing, spritz liberally with water and steam-press with a firm hand.

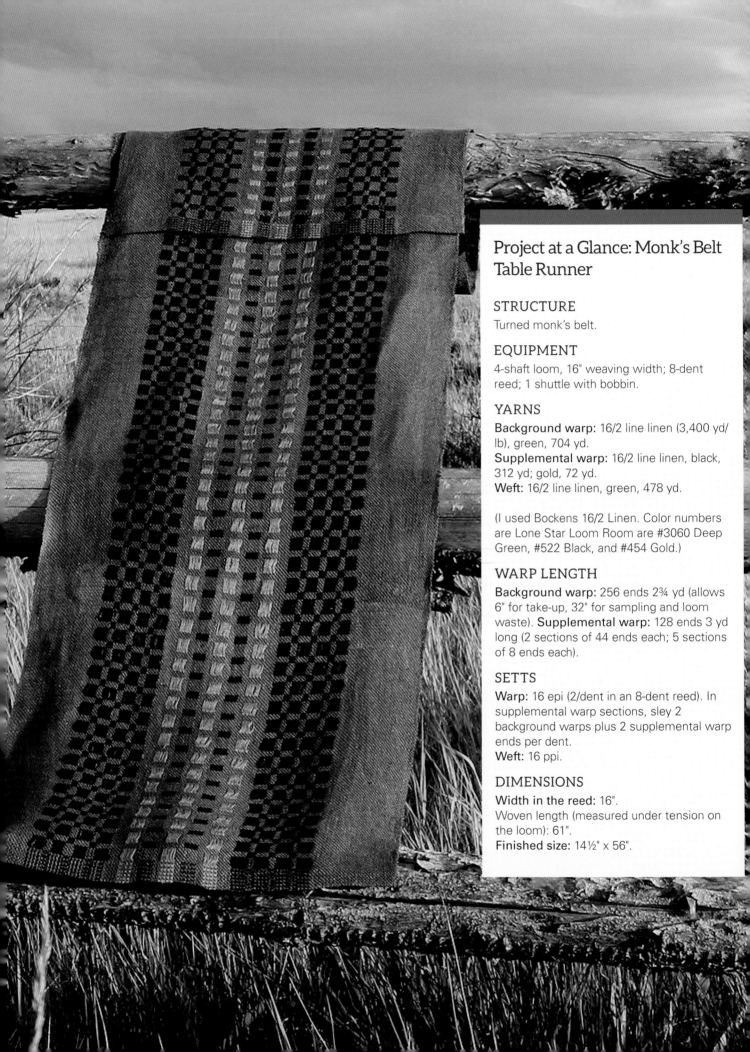

Project at a Glance: Monk's Belt Table Runner

STRUCTURE
Turned monk's belt.

EQUIPMENT
4-shaft loom, 16" weaving width; 8-dent reed; 1 shuttle with bobbin.

YARNS
Background warp: 16/2 line linen (3,400 yd/lb), green, 704 yd.
Supplemental warp: 16/2 line linen, black, 312 yd; gold, 72 yd.
Weft: 16/2 line linen, green, 478 yd.

(I used Bockens 16/2 Linen. Color numbers are Lone Star Loom Room are #3060 Deep Green, #522 Black, and #454 Gold.)

WARP LENGTH
Background warp: 256 ends 2¾ yd (allows 6" for take-up, 32" for sampling and loom waste). **Supplemental warp:** 128 ends 3 yd long (2 sections of 44 ends each; 5 sections of 8 ends each).

SETTS
Warp: 16 epi (2/dent in an 8-dent reed). In supplemental warp sections, sley 2 background warps plus 2 supplemental warp ends per dent.
Weft: 16 ppi.

DIMENSIONS
Width in the reed: 16".
Woven length (measured under tension on the loom): 61".
Finished size: 14½" x 56".

STEP BY STEP INSTRUCTIONS

Step 1 Wind 256 warp threads 23/4 yd long of the background warp. Wind 7 separate supplemental warp bouts 3 yd long: 2 bouts of black of, 44 threads each; 3 bouts of gold, 8 threads each; and 2 bouts of black, 8 threads each. Set the supplemental warp bouts aside. Thread the background warps according to the directions in Chapter 2, following the draft in Figure 1.

Step 2 Wind the three supplemental warp chains. Spritz all the warp chains with water and let them air dry.

Step 3 Lay supplemental warps on the loom as described in Chapter 2. Thread the supplemental warps on shafts 1 and 2 following the draft for colors. Space the supplemental warps across the background warp as follows:

Step 4 Start the first supplemental warp 48 background warp ends (3") from the edge. Bundle the background warp threads in 1" groups, tie with scrap yarn or hair ties, and push all 3 to the side. Thread the first supplemental warp chain according to the draft, with 1 background warp thread between supplemental warp yarns. There should be a total of 44 background warps and 48 supplemental warps in the first section.

Step 5 Count out 8 background warps and push to the side, then thread the five small supplemental warp chains according to the draft. As you work, bundle each supplemental warp section with its background threads and push to the side.

Step 6 Thread the second large black warp chain as you did the first. When you finish, there should be 48 background warp threads left for background cloth to selvedge

Step 7 Sley the reed, centering for a 16" weaving width. There will be 2 ends/dent in the background-only areas. The supplemental warp sections will have 2 background warp ends and 2 supplemental warp ends per dent.

Step 8 Tie on using your preferred method, including the pattern warps with the background warp in the tie-on groups. Weight the supplemental warp bouts over the back beam. Adjust your background warp tension to match that provided by the weights. (Add weight if you like to weave with more tension).

Step 9 Wind a bobbin of weft yarn. Weave a few picks of scrap yarn to spread the warp. Weave 2" of plain weave for a hem. Weave the scarf following the treadling repeat in the draft for 57", then weave 2" of plain weave for the other hem. Weave a few picks of scrap yarn to protect the edge.

Step 10 Machine zig-zag across both ends to secure wefts and warps. Remove all scrap yarns.

Step 11 Wash in very warm water with mild detergent. Rinse. Toss in the dryer with a towel and dry until slightly damp or lay flat until almost dry. Set iron to high steam and heat, and press firmly. If the runner gets completely dry in the dryer, spritz it liberally with water before pressing.

Figure 1. Draft

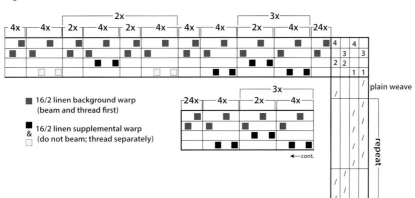

Monk's Belt Placemats

Traditional monk's belt (selvedge-to-selvedge float blocks) isn't one of my favorite weave structures, **but** as a supplemental warp, monk's belt has stolen my weaving heart. The variety of designs I can create on just four shafts is so addicting! For the revised version of this book, I had to include more monk's belt projects.

Originally, I sampled the pattern design in traditional monk's belt. I tired quickly of juggling shuttles and wasn't thrilled with how the cotton pattern floats behaved at the selvedges. But as turned monk's belt, I need only one shuttle, don't need to worry about floating selvedges or floppy pattern wefts, and can easily use multiple colors in the supplemental warp pattern bands. Bonus: these placemats weave up fast!

Project at a Glance: Monk's Belt Placemats

STRUCTURE
Turned monk's belt

EQUIPMENT
4-shaft loom, 14" weaving width, 8 dent reed, 1 shuttle with bobbin

YARNS
(all yarn yardages are to weave 2 placemats)
Background warp: 5/2 pearl cotton (2,100 yds/lb; Lunatic Fringe Tubular Spectrum), Forest, 504 yds
Supplemental warp: 5/2 pearl cotton, Green-Yellow, 160 yds; Copper, 187 yds
Weft: 5/2 pearl cotton, Forest and Cobalt Blue, 136 yds each

WARP LENGTH
Background warp: 224 ends at 2¼ yd (allows 45" for take-up allowance, 33" for loom waste and sampling)
Supplemental warp: Green-Yellow, 58 ends 2¼ yd Copper, 68 ends 2¼ yd

Warp: 16 epi. (Sley 2 ends/dent in 8-dent reed.) In supplemental warp sections, sley 2 background warps and 2 supplemental warps per dent.
Weft: 16 ppi.

DIMENSIONS
Width in reed: 14"
Woven length (measured under tension on the loom): 43" (includes two 20" placemats plus 3" to spread the warp).
Finished size (washed and hemmed): 16" x 12½".

SETTS

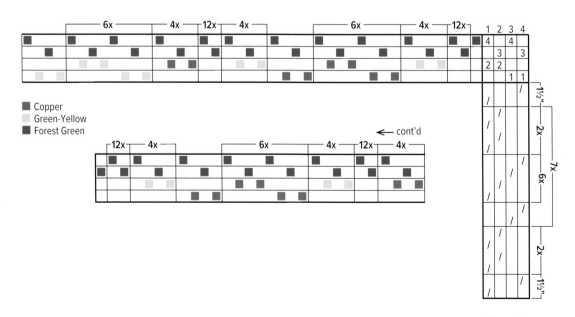

■ Copper
■ Green-Yellow
■ Forest Green

Figure 1

STEP BY STEP INSTRUCTIONS

Step 1   Wind 244 warp ends 2¼ yd long for background warp. Thread the background warps according to the directions in Chapter 2, following the draft in in Figure 1. Count 24 background warp threads for the border from the right selvedge and bundle with a piece of thrum yarn.

Step 2   Wind three supplemental warp chains each 2¾ yd long as follows:

Supplemental warp bouts # 1 and #3: 16 ends Green-Yellow, 26 ends Copper, 16 ends Green-Yellow.

Supplemental warp bout #2: 16 ends Copper, 26 ends Green-Yellow, 16 ends Copper.

Step 3   Lay the supplemental warps on the loom as described in Chapter 2, with the contrasting bout #2 in between bouts 1 and 3.

Step 4   Starting *after* the 24 background warps you bundled in step 1, thread the first supplemental warp according to the draft in Figure 1. The supplemental warps go on shafts 1 and 2 with one background warp between every supplemental warp thread.

Step 5   After threading supplemental bout #1, count 24 background threads and bundle them. Thread supplemental bout #2. Count another 24 background threads and bundle. Thread supplemental bout #3. There should be 24 background threads remaining.

TIP: These supplemental warps are each about three inches width, and as mentioned in Chapter 2, two inches is really the maximum width to help with tensioning the warps. To solve this, place your cross counting thread for **each full** supplement warp chain. When you place the **choke ties and end ties**, split each supplemental warp chain into two bouts. This gives you two sections per supplemental warp chain, each about one and a half inches wide, and you can hang weights on **each half** of the warp chain. Trust me, this will make a difference.

Step 6   Sley the reed. All sections with *only background* threads are sleyed two ends/dent. Sections with background and supplemental warps are sleyed two background and two supplemental warps per dent.

Step 7   Tie on, using your preferred method, including the supplemental pattern threads with the background threads in the tie-on groups. Weight each section of the supplemental warp bouts to tension.

Step 8   To even out the warps and test tension, weave 2–3" of warp with waste yarn.

Step 9   Wind a bobbin with the first weft color and weave 1½" of plain weave for the hem. Weave 17" of pattern, ending with a complete pattern, using a firm beat. (Depending on your beat, this may be anywhere from 16½" to 17¼"). End by weaving 1½" of plain weave for hem.

If you have trouble with the supplemental warp threads not moving cleanly when they switch fabric sides, you can add weight to the supplemental warps, back off a notch on the background warp tension, and/or give a sharp beat each time you change sheds to pop any stuck warps to the correct position.

Step 10   Wind a bobbin with the second weft color. Weave two picks of waste yarn. This marks the cutting line between placemats. Weave the second placemat. End with a couple of picks of waste yarn to lock the fell line. Cut placemats off the loom.

Step 11   With a sewing machine, zigzag stitch across each end of the placemats. Remove waste yarns at both ends, but don't cut placemats apart yet. Soak the placemats in warm water and lay flat to dry. I've found hand washing and drying flat for the first wash reduces shrinkage when the placemats are machine washed and dried in the future. Cut the placemats apart between the two picks of waste yarn for a perfectly straight cut. Hem: Turn the ends under ¼" and press. Match the folded edge to the end of the pattern. Press and pin. Machine or handstitch the folded edges to the body of the placemat—invite someone to dinner!

Photo by Chris Autio

Koani's Turned Monk's Belt Scarf

This monk's belt design uses knitting yarn for the supplemental warps. If you look closely at the picture, the designs look a bit rounded. The DK weight yarn (refer to yarn chart on page 42) used for the supplemental warp threads are much larger than the lace weight background warp but the supplemental yarn also has a high "squishability" factor (see page 41). However, the amount of yarn in each pattern section makes the pattern blocks appear slightly rounded. Think of it as trying to pack a soft-sided bag. The more you items stuff into the bag, the farther out the sides will bulge. The same thing happens with a large supplemental warp yarn: the pattern sections can bulge out at the sides because the yarns take up more space. Now, I like the softer, rounded pattern, so it's in the book. If you like the look, follow the draft as written.

But what if you prefer a more squared design? You have a couple options. Option 1: Use a smaller grist knitting yarn such as Fingering or Sport weight yarn for the supplemental warps. Then follow the draft as written. Option 2: Use a larger yarn but fewer supplemental warp ends. To accommodate the larger grist/size of the supplemental warps you: (a) Reduce the number of supplemental warp ends in each pattern block by half. If there are 4 supplemental warp threads in a block, you would wind 2 supplemental warp threads instead of 4. You still wind the total number of background warp threads, but now have 2 background threads for every 1 supplemental warp thread. (b) When you pull the supplemental warp threads through the background threads you will push over 2 background threads between each supplemental warp thread. (c) When sleying, you sley two background warp threads with one supplemental warp thread per dent, which spreads the supplemental warp threads over a larger area of the background. Note: I highly recommend doing samples to test your yarn sizes/spacing before doing a big project! Knitting yarns can vary in size even in the same "weight classes".

You may wonder why this project is named "Koani's Scarf" (pronounced Ko-WAN-ee). The supplemental warp yarns are very special—the yarn is a custom spun blend of wolf down and Merino wool. The wolf down was supplied by Koani, a gray wolf who lived with my good friends Pat and Bruce for sixteen years in the 1990s into the early 2000s. Pat is a wildlife biologist specializing in wolves and was part of the reintroduction of wolves into Yellowstone National Park in 1995. Pat also consulted for a documentary film about wolves, and Koani was one of the "stars" as a tiny pup. Because Koani had been habituated to humans, her future was bleak—life in a zoo or euthanasia. Pat and Bruce came up with a third option: create a nonprofit and have Koani help educate humans about wolves.

Together, Pat, Bruce, Koani, and Indy (Koani's faithful domestic canine companion) traveled the United States in an RV, teaching in schools, museums, and nature centers. Like domestic dogs, wolves shed their soft winter undercoat each spring. For years, Pat brushed Koani's coat and saved the undercoat fiber. A few years after Koani died at age 16, Pat had yarn spun at a small fiber mill in Montana, blending the wolf down with wool from a friend's Merino ewe. I made two of these scarves—one for Pat, one for Bruce.

Dog undercoat fiber is easier for the rest of us to come by—so if you have been saving your dog's undercoat for some future project, this could be it!

Project at a Glance: Koani's Turned Monk's Belt Scarf

STRUCTURE
Turned monk's belt

EQUIPMENT
4-shaft loom, 9" weaving width, 8 dent reed, 1 shuttle with bobbin

YARNS
Background warp: 18/2 lace weight wool/silk (1,120 yds/100 gm skein, Jaggerspun Zephyr), Ebony, 396 yds
Supplemental warps: DK weight knitting yarn, gray, 144 yds
Weft: 18/2 lace weight wool/silk, Ebony, 290 yds

WARP LENGTH
Background warp: 144 ends 2¾ yds long at 94" long (allows 6" for take-up and 28" for loom waste; loom waste includes frings).
Supplemental warps: 3 bouts; 12, 24, and 12 ends, 3 yds long.

SETTS
Warp: 16 epi (2 threads/dent in an 8-dent reed). In supplemental warp sections, sley 2 background warps and two supplement warps per dent.
Weft: 16 ppi

DIMENSIONS
Width in reed: 9"
Woven length: 65" or closest measurement to complete pattern repeat (measured off tension on the loom)
Finished size: 8.5" wide by 60" long

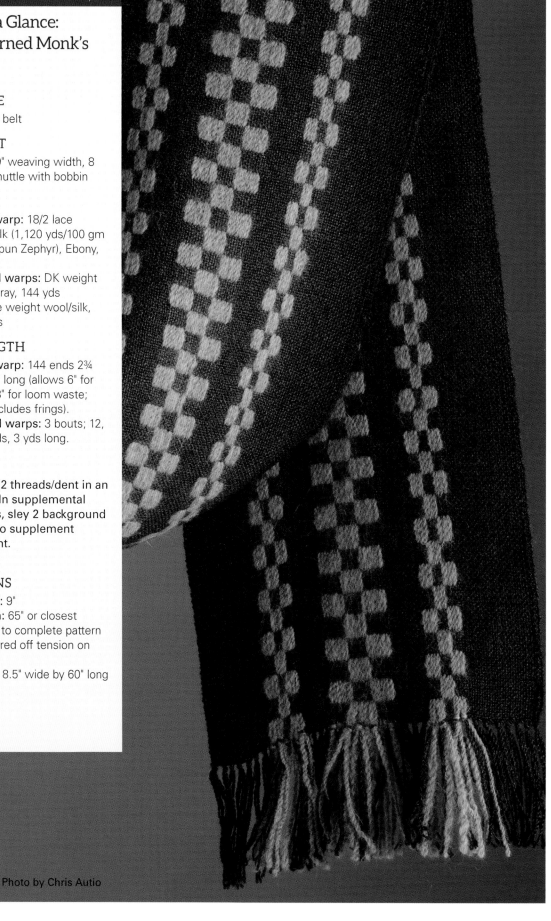

Photo by Chris Autio

Figure 1

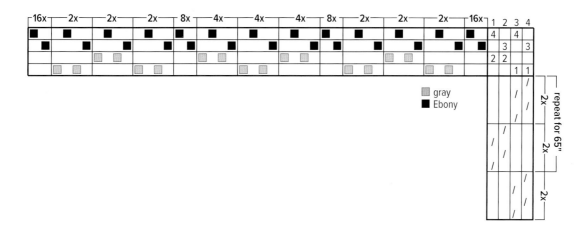

STEP BY STEP INSTRUCTIONS

Step 1   Wind 144 warp threads 3 yds long of the background warp yarn. Thread the background threads according to the directions in Chapter 2, following the draft in Figure 1.

Step 2   Wind three supplemental warp chains. Warp #1 is 12 ends, warp #2 is 24 ends, and warp #3 is 12 ends.

Step 3   Lay the supplemental warps on the loom as described in Chapter 2. Thread the supplemental warps: Count out 32 background warp threads from the right-hand side, bundle with a piece of thrum yarn, and push to the side. Thread supplemental warp #1 on shafts 1 and 2 following the draft. You will thread 1 supplemental thread then pull through 1 background thread in each section of supplemental warp pattern. There are 16 background threads between each section of supplemental warp pattern and you will have 32 background warp threads on the left selvedge edge.

Step 4   Sley the reed, centering for 9" weaving width. For background warp sections, sley two ends per dent. When you reach the supplemental warp sections, sley two background and two supplemental warps per dent.

Step 5   Separate the background warp from the supplemental warps and tie on the background warps first, using your preferred method. Tie the supplemental warps to the apron rod, using the shoelace method shown in Chapter 2, Photo 22. Weight each supplemental warp at the back of the loom.

Step 6   Weave 6" of waste yarn for the scarf's fringe. Adjust the weight on the supplemental warps when weaving the fringe section if necessary. (See "Troubleshooting" section at the end of Chapter 2.)

Step 7   Wind a bobbin with the weft yarn. Start weaving using the pattern treadling in the draft. Weave 65", making sure to balance your pattern in the supplemental warp sections. When you reach the finished length, weave a few picks of waste yarn to protect the end. Cut the scarf off the loom so you have 6" of warp length to use for fringe.

Step 8   Remove the waste yarn on one end of the scarf. Tie overhand knots in bundles of four warp ends across the end of the scarf. Repeat this step for the other end of the scarf.

Step 9   Hand wash in warm water and lay flat to dry. Trim the fringe ends so they are even. Enjoy!

Turned Overshot Scarf

TURNED OVERSHOT IS BY FAR MY FAVORITE supplemental warp structure. I can highlight sections of a traditional overshot design that I like and sometimes leave out a section that I don't like. It's also a wonderful way to incorporate a small amount of handspun yarn or expensive yarn that could break my budget in traditional overshot.

Chapter 1 examines in depth how to turn overshot drafts. Please read through that section before charging into this project. Remember that the draft for the project is a shorthand draft and shows the threading for both background warps and supplemental warps in the first section only. Remember that the background warps continue to be added between supplemental warps in every supplemental warp section as shown in the first supplemental warp threading section.

The supplemental warp yarn for this project, by Blue Heron yarns, is a handpainted cotton yarn plied with shiny rayon. I fell in love with the colors, consistent color changes, and shiny highlights, but when I tried to use it as a plain-weave warp, the color changes and highlights were overwhelmed by the weft. As a plain-weave weft, the color repeats created small stripes that didn't please me. Turned overshot to the rescue! The supplemental warp overshot pattern and the plain-weave background cloth highlight the color changes and iridescence in this yarn.

The overshot design is a name draft I created based on the words "I weave." Name drafts are secret messages woven in cloth. The letters of the alphabet are assigned to the shafts of the loom to create a code key. You create the pattern using the letters in a word, name, or phrase, and thread the warp threads on the shafts according to the code key to create a unique pattern. For example: In the full version of this draft in regular overshot, the letter "I" is assigned to shaft 1, so the first thread is on shaft 1. "W" is on shaft 3, so I thread on shaft 3.

Project at a Glance: Turned Overshot Scarf

STRUCTURE
Turned overshot.

EQUIPMENT
6-shaft loom, 8" weaving width; 10-dent reed; 1 shuttle with bobbin.

YARNS
Background warp: 8/2 Tencel (3,360 yd/lb), navy blue, 480 yd.
Supplemental warp: laceweight knitting yarn, space-dyed, 134 yd.
Weft: 8/2 Tencel, navy blue, 352 yd.

(I used 8/2 Tencel from WEBS in Navy for background warp and weft, and Blue Heron Yarns Twist Lace (cotton/rayon; 1,000 yd/skein) in the Water Hyacinth colorway for the supplementary warp.)

WARP LENGTH
Background warp: 160 ends 3 yd long (allows 7" for take-up, 29" for sampling and loom waste; loom waste includes fringe). **Supplemental warp:** 41 ends 3¼ yd long (1 section).

SETTS
Warp: 20 epi (2/dent in a 10-dent reed). In supplemental warp sections, sley 2 background warps plus 2 supplemental warp ends per dent.
Weft: 20 ppi.

DIMENSIONS
Width in the reed: 8".
Woven length (measured under tension on the loom): 72".
Finished size: 7¼" x 66" plus fringe.

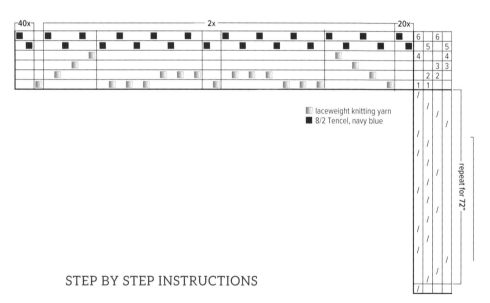

laceweight knitting yarn
8/2 Tencel, navy blue

repeat for 72"

STEP BY STEP INSTRUCTIONS

Step 1 Wind 160 warp threads 3 yd long of the background warp. Wind 1 supplemental warp bout 31/4 yd long. Set the supplemental warp bouts aside.

Step 2 Thread the background warps according to the directions in Chapter 2, following the draft in Figure 1.

Step 3 Lay supplemental warps on the loom as described in Chapter 2. Thread the supplemental warps on shafts 1 and 2 following the draft for colors. Then count 40 background warp ends from the right selvedge,

bundle, and push aside. Thread the supplemental warp bundle according to the draft, with one back with 1 background warp thread between supplemental warp ends. When you finish threading, there should be 80 background warp threads remaining to the other selvedge. (The stripe is not centered in the scarf.)

Step 4   Sley the reed, centering for an 8" weaving width. There will be 2 ends/dent in the background-only areas. The supplemental warp sections will have 2 background warp ends and 2 supplemental warp ends per dent, except for the last supplemental warp end, which will be in a dent with 2 background warp ends.

Step 5   Tie on using your preferred method, including the pattern warps with the background warp in the tie-on groups. Weight the supplemental warp bouts over the back beam. Adjust your background warp tension to match that provided by the weights. (Add weight if you like to weave with more tension).

Step 6   Wind a bobbin of weft yarn. Weave at least 5" of waste yarn or rags for the fringes and to help even out the supplemental warp. (Weave more if you want longer fringes.) This is also the time to check that the supplemental warp has the proper amount of weight. Weave the scarf following the treadling repeat in the draft for 72", and finish with a few picks of scrap yarn or rag to protect the ends.

Step 7   Cut scarf off the loom, leaving at least 5" at the end for fringe. Remove scrap yarns when you make fringe at each end. Tie fringe in overhand knots firmly against the ends. In ground cloth-only areas, tie bundles of 4 ends per knot. In the supplemental warp section, tie 4 ends of background and 4 ends of supplemental warp in each knot.

Step 8   Handwash in warm water and lay flat to dry. The Tencel yarn will feel stiff after washing. Don't worry: it will soften up beautifully once dry.

Step 9   Trim fringes to desired length and enjoy!

"I Weave" Turned Overshot Shawl

Shortly after the original version of this book was published, a weaver asked me if it's possible to do multiple overshot patterns selvedge to selvedge in different colors. Well, yes, it's more than possible and great fun!

I wove this shawl for the Leader's Exhibit at Handweavers Guild of America (HGA) Convergence conference in Reno, Nevada, in 2018. In my spinning fiber stash I had two packages of yak/silk roving dyed by Greenwood Fiberworks, each containing five different colors in 1-ounce braids. I spun up the roving, using a short (worsted) draw, then Navajo-plied it into a 3-ply fingering weight yarn. I wound up with about 130 yards of yarn in each color. I didn't have a lot of yardage in each color, but I decided that if planned carefully, I'd be able to weave an infinity shawl showcasing the yarns and the "I weave" overshot name draft in this book. It's the perfect project for those special little skeins of handspun in your stash (or any other special yarn of which you have a limited supply).

This shawl uses the same "I Weave" turned overshot name draft as the previous scarf. However, instead of one repeat of the overshot pattern, it uses seven repeats of pattern, one for each skein/color of yarn.

Project at a Glance:
"I Weave" Turned Overshot Shawl

STRUCTURE
Turned overshot

EQUIPMENT
6-shaft loom with 24" weaving width; 8-dent reed; 1 shuttle with bobbin

YARNS
18/2 wool/silk (1,120 yds per 100 gm skein; Jaggerspun Zephyr), Ebony, 946 yds

Supplemental warp: Fingering weight knitting yarn or similar weight weaving yarn (or your handspun yarn!), 120 yds for each color (2 pattern repeats) of turned overshot pattern, 123 yds for final color.

Weft: 18/2 wool/silk lace weight yarn, Ebony, 705 yds

WARP LENGTH
Background warp: 344 ends 2¾ yds long (allows for 6" for take-up, 26" for loom waste)

Supplemental warps: 6 bouts 40 ends 3 yds long, 1 bout 41 ends 3 yrds. long. Each supplemental warp bout is 2.5" wide.

SETT
Warp: 16 epi 2 dent in 8-dent reed. In supplemental warp sections, sley 2 background warp threads and 2 supplemental warp threads in each dent.
Weft: 16 ppi

DIMENSIONS
Width in the reed: 21½"
Woven length (measured under tension on the loom): 67"
Finished size (before joining ends): 20" x 63"

Figure 1

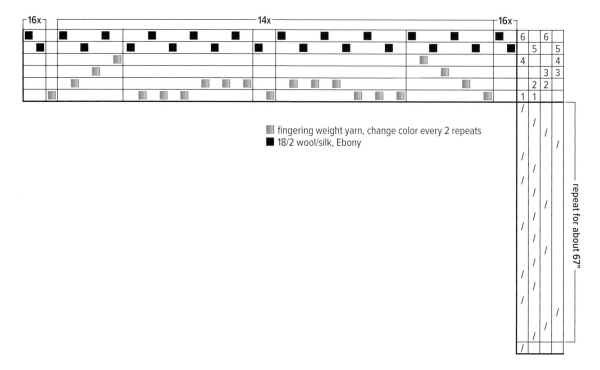

fingering weight yarn, change color every 2 repeats
18/2 wool/silk, Ebony

STEP BY STEP INSTRUCTIONS

Step 1 Wind 344 ends 2¾ yds long of the background warp.

Step 2 Thread the background warp threads according to the directions in Chapter 2, following the draft in Figure 1.

Step 3 Wind 6 supplemental warp bouts of 40 warp ends each, and one bout of 41 ends for the last color. Each bout should have its own choke ties, end ties, counting thread at the cross, and cross papers.

Step 4 Count 32 background warp threads from the right selvedge and bundle with a small piece of thrum. Push bundle aside to the right. Count 32 warp threads from the *left* selvedge, bundle, and push aside to the left. These bundles will be the plain-weave edges of the shawl. Because there are an odd number of total supplemental warp ends (6 repeats x 40 threads plus 1 repeat of 41 threads = 281), the last supplemental warp thread will be in the space between the threaded supplemental warps and the bundle of 32 ends for the left border. It will be sleyed with the first two background warp threads for the left-hand border section.

Step 5 Lay the supplemental warps on the loom as directed in Chapter 2, so that all bundles lie next to each other, starting and ending at the points where the plain weave borders are on each side.

Step 6 Thread the supplemental warp threads on shafts 1–4, using the draft in Figure 1 with one background thread between every supplemental warp thread. Repeat the pattern section in the draft for each bundle of supplemental warp threads, with one background thread between the supplemental warp bouts.

Step 7 Sley the reed. In the borders of background threads only, sley two background warp ends per dent until you reach the supplemental warps. Now sley two background warps and two supplemental warps per dent. When you reach the other border, return to sleying two background warps per dent.

Step 8 Tie on, using your preferred method, including the pattern warps with the background warps in the tie-on bundles. Weight the supplemental warp bouts over the back beam.

Step 9 Wind a bobbin with the background weft yarn. Weave about 2" with waste yarn or rags to even out the supplemental warps. (You may have to add more weights or wrap the warps around the dowel at the back beam for tension. See Photo 25 in Chapter 1). Weave the scarf following the treadling repeat in Figure 1 for 657" or as close as possible, completing the last repeat.

Step 10 Cut shawl off the loom. Zigzag stitch the ends, then remove the waste yarn.

Step 11 Handwash in warm water and lay flat to dry.

Step 12 To make the twisted infinity scarf: Trim the excess warp ends close to the zigzag stitching on each end. Turn up one end ½" (so you see the raw edge) and press. Turn the opposite end under ½" (you see only the folded edge) and press. Laying the shawl flat, fold back one end about a foot. Now, take the other end and twist the length ½" turn. Bring the two ends together and pin together along the folded edge so the raw edges are tucked inside the layers of fabric. Hem by hand all edges. Enjoy!

Turned Overshot Diamonds Infinity Scarf

I love classic overshot designs woven with multiple weft colors, but it involves a lot of shuttle juggling! It's so much easier with supplemental warp. For a long time, the idea of using Mountain Colors "Perspective" **Twizzlefoot** sock yarn, sets of five 85-yard skeins dyed in coordinating colors, perked in my brain. I've woven a lot of supplemental warp fabrics, but this project taught me some new lessons! I've added it to the revised version of the book, so that when you try turned overshot in multiple colors, you don't have to learn the same lessons the hard way. Forewarned is forearmed!

Lesson 1—I consulted my copy of Marguerite Porter Davison's *A Handweaver's Pattern Book* for classic overshot designs with strong pattern repeats. On page 156, a striking diamond design called "John Madison" caught my eye. A quick count of the block repeats confirmed that I could use all five colors across the design. I entered one repeat of the pattern into my weaving program and used the "Turn Draft" command. Then I played with the warp color sequence and settled on the color progression/proportions in this draft.

Lesson 2—Winding the supplemental warp chains: Each color block is 14 ends, and the orange "divider designs" are seven ends each. I wound the supplemental warps next to each other, placing end ties, choke ties, and papers on both sides of each cross as I normally do. (See Chapter 2 on winding supplemental warps.) Then I chained each supplemental warp individually and realized it was not going to be easy inserting lease sticks at the loom through all these very narrow warp chains. Instead, I laid the warps on the floor in color order, inserted lease sticks on both sides of the cross, removed all those papers, and slowly, carefully brought the whole thing to the loom. Miraculously, I didn't drop the sticks, step on a warp, or have any other potential disaster, and I secured the lease sticks without losing the cross. (See "Step by Step Instructions" for a much better procedure. Trust me.)

Note: When creating pieces where the supplemental warps go almost selvedge to selvedge, I've found it's very important not to take the supplemental warp sections to the very edge of the background warp. Leave at least ¼" of background cloth on each selvedge, or the supplemental pattern designs will distort at the edges.

Lesson 3—Sock knitting yarn is designed to stretch. Good for socks, tricky for weaving. I got everything threaded and tied on, and then I weighted each individual color bout of yarn. I wove a bit of waste yarn, and things looked great! Then I started to weave the pattern with the 8/2 Tencel, and I noticed the supplemental yarns weren't always moving cleanly between the sides of the fabric. The sock yarn was literally bending around the background warp threads instead of moving cleanly to the other side. I wound the wider warps around the dowel on the back beam, pulled the warps to a firm tension, and weighted *each* 14-end supplemental warp bout with 16 ounces of weight. I didn't wrap 7-end warp bouts around the dowel, and I only weighted them with 6 ounces. And still sometimes the yarns would catch when transitioning to a new block. I discovered that opening the next shed and doing a quick, sharp beat with the shed open would pop the stuck warps to the correct side.

STEP BY STEP INSTRUCTIONS

Step 1 Wind 144 warp threads 2½ yds long of the background warp. Thread the background warps according to directions in Chapter 2, following the draft in Figure 1.

Step 2 Wind 11 supplemental warps 88" long next to each other on the warping board as shown in Figure 2.

With so many narrow sections of supplemental warps (see "Lessons" at beginning of project), I suggest a slightly different way of securing the warps. As you wind the individual colors, tie choke ties for *each color* section of warp so the choke ties line up with each other (see photo 16 in Chapter 2). Use end ties on *each end of each section* of supplemental warp. Bundle each color section with the counting thread at the cross so all sections are *bundled by color,* using only one counting thread. Insert two lease stick papers, one on each side of the cross, so the papers encompass the *entire* warp width. Do *not* use individual sets of papers for each supplemental warp chain.

Step 3 Lay the supplemental warps on the loom and insert the lease sticks on each side of the cross. Remove the cross papers and the counting thread. Spread the supplemental warps across the width of the background warps.

Step 4 Edge-to-edge designs work best when you start threading the supplemental warps about ¼" in from the selvedges. Count six background warp ends at the selvedge and bundle. Now thread the supplemental warps according to the draft in Figure 1, with one background warp thread between each supplemental warp thread. There will be six background warps left when you finish threading the supplemental warps.

Step 5 Sley the reed, centering for width of 7-3/10". Sley the first six background warps two ends/dent. Then sley two background warps and two supplemental warps per dent across. Because there are an odd number (133) of total supplemental warp ends, the last supplemental warp end will be sleyed with two background warp threads. Sley the remaining background warps 2 ends/dent.

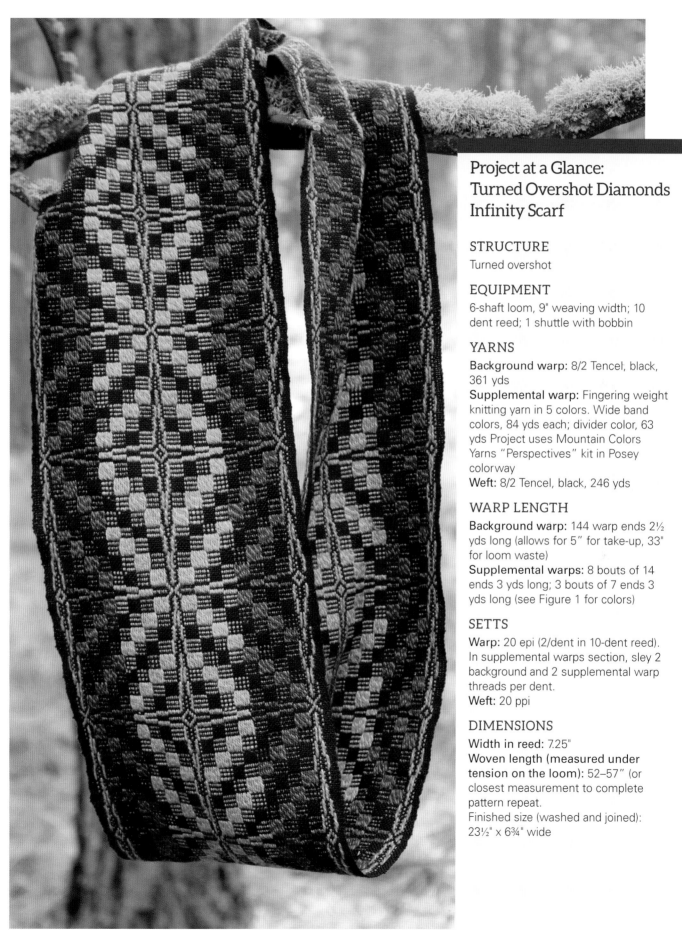

Project at a Glance: Turned Overshot Diamonds Infinity Scarf

STRUCTURE
Turned overshot

EQUIPMENT
6-shaft loom, 9" weaving width; 10 dent reed; 1 shuttle with bobbin

YARNS
Background warp: 8/2 Tencel, black, 361 yds
Supplemental warp: Fingering weight knitting yarn in 5 colors. Wide band colors, 84 yds each; divider color, 63 yds Project uses Mountain Colors Yarns "Perspectives" kit in Posey colorway
Weft: 8/2 Tencel, black, 246 yds

WARP LENGTH
Background warp: 144 warp ends 2½ yds long (allows for 5" for take-up, 33" for loom waste)
Supplemental warps: 8 bouts of 14 ends 3 yds long; 3 bouts of 7 ends 3 yds long (see Figure 1 for colors)

SETTS
Warp: 20 epi (2/dent in 10-dent reed). In supplemental warps section, sley 2 background and 2 supplemental warp threads per dent.
Weft: 20 ppi

DIMENSIONS
Width in reed: 7.25"
Woven length (measured under tension on the loom): 52–57" (or closest measurement to complete pattern repeat.
Finished size (washed and joined): 23½" x 6¾" wide

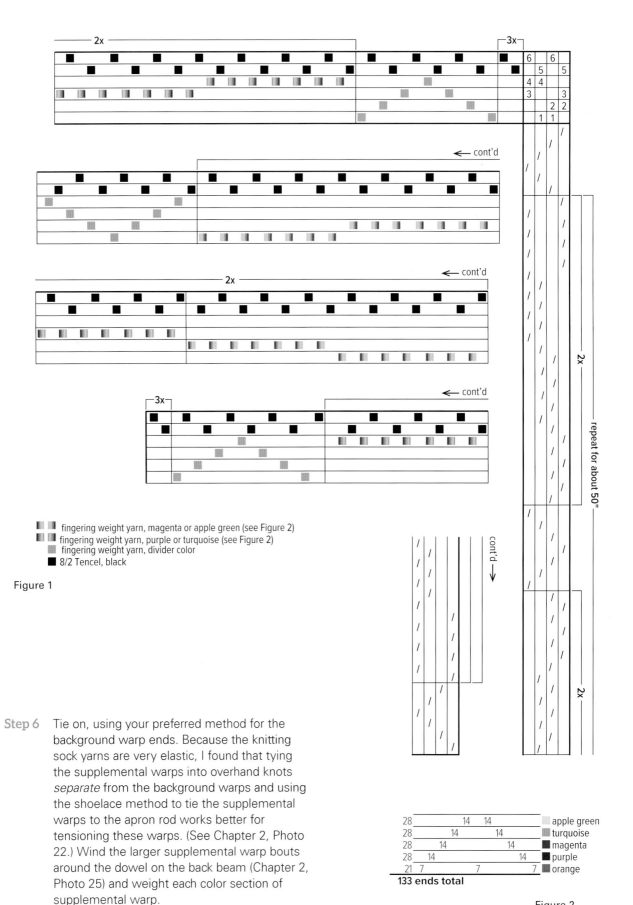

fingering weight yarn, magenta or apple green (see Figure 2)
fingering weight yarn, purple or turquoise (see Figure 2)
fingering weight yarn, divider color
8/2 Tencel, black

Figure 1

28			14	14		apple green
28		14			14	turquoise
28		14			14	magenta
28	14				14	purple
21	7		7		7	orange

133 ends total

Figure 2

Step 6 Tie on, using your preferred method for the background warp ends. Because the knitting sock yarns are very elastic, I found that tying the supplemental warps into overhand knots *separate* from the background warps and using the shoelace method to tie the supplemental warps to the apron rod works better for tensioning these warps. (See Chapter 2, Photo 22.) Wind the larger supplemental warp bouts around the dowel on the back beam (Chapter 2, Photo 25) and weight each color section of supplemental warp.

Step 7 Wind a bobbin with weft yarn. Weave 2"–3" of waste yarn to even out the warps and test tension on the supplemental warps. Weave five full repeats of the treadling for about 50", making sure to complete the treadling sequence for a full pattern repeat, with the final repeat ending with the seven point-twill picks to complete the pattern. Weave a few picks of waste yarn to protect the end.

Step 8 Cut the scarf off the loom. Zigzag stitch the ends. Remove waste yarns. Hand wash in warm water and lay flat to dry.

Step 9 Trim the warp ends close to the zigzag stitching. Turn under one end ¼" to the top of the fabric, press. Turn the other end of the scarf ¼" to the back side of the fabric. Bring the two ends together without twisting, so that the folded ends overlap and the raw edges are enclosed. Hem by hand around all edges of join. Go out on the town!

Bedford Cord

IF WEAVE STRUCTURES WERE RELATIVES, Bedford cord would be a first cousin of two-block doubleweave. Like doubleweave, Bedford cord consists of two layers of fabric. Unlike doubleweave, which creates a reversible fabric, Bedford cord is a one-sided fabric with plain weave on the right side of the fabric and weft floats on the back that create a ridged or ribbed structure running the length of the cloth. Because it is one-sided, Bedford cord is good for projects such as upholstery, rugs, woven trivets, and table runners, in which only the right side of the cloth is visible. You can also fold the fabric so the float side is concealed for items like potholders or pillow covers.

Bedford cord also allows weft yarns to interlace with selected stripes running the length of the fabric. To help wrap our heads around this idea, let's compare Bedford cord to a plain-weave striped fabric. To create length-wise stripes in only one layer of cloth, you wind the warp in sections of different colors and/or yarns. If you weave with only one color of weft, the interlacement of the warp and weft creates vertical stripes that are either a blend of the weft yarn color and warp stripe color or a solid color stripe where the warp and weft are the same color. With Bedford cord, you can control whether the weft thread is weaving only the top fabric layer or the only the bottom fabric layer, and thus you can make the wefts interlace only with the same color of warp. This allows you to weave solid color stripes in multiple colors across the entire width and length of the fabric. And that's only the beginning! Let's dive into this in more detail.

Bedford cord requires four shafts to weave two blocks of plain weave. It requires a closer sett than normal plain weave in order to keep the weft floats on the back of the fabric. A firmer sett also helps define the ribs on the cloth face. Use a slightly closer sett than you would normally use for plain weave in your chosen yarn, and sample to make sure it works.

The two blocks of plain weave in this project alternate threading on shafts 1 and 2 (block A) with threading on shafts 3 and 4 (block B), an odd-even sequence that lends itself to plain weave. The rib and float patterning happens in the tie-up. Looking at the draft in Figure 1, you can see that the *warp* is threaded in alternating orange and blue stripes, orange on shafts 1 and 2 and blue on shafts 3 and 4. If you look at the tie-up and treadling, you'll see that the first and third picks lift the odd and then even shaft of block A (shafts 1 and then 2), with shafts 3 and 4 (block B) lifted on both picks, so that the weft will float on the bottom of the cloth. The second and fourth picks are the two plain-weave picks of block B, with the block A shafts lifted to create floats on the back of the cloth. You'll also see that all weft threads that interlace with shafts 1 and 2 are orange and all *weft* treads that interlace with shafts 3 and 4 are blue, making the colors alternate in solid stripes across the fabric. These are the ribs that show on the right side of the cloth. In each stripe, the opposite weft color is floating on the back of the cloth.

Photo 1. Close up photo of Bedford cord sample showing both front and back sides of the fabric

As with doubleweave, we alternate weaving a pick in block A with a pick in block B so that weft doesn't build up in one rib, preventing a good beat in the second rib **(see Photo 1 and Figure 1)**.

I recommend arranging your treadles so that treadles 1 and 2 are pressed with your left foot and treadles 3 and 4 are pressed with your right foot. Leave a couple of open treadles between treadles 2 and 3. This makes it easy to find the correct treadle as you weave.

The difference in draw-in between the plain-weave top and the bottom layer, where the wefts merrily skip across the warp ends, causes the fabric to bump up into a rib that runs the length of the cloth when the fabric is removed from the loom. The ribs can be any width you want, but keep in mind that the farther the weft floats travel underneath the ribs, the less cohesive the fabric and the less dramatic the rib structure. In addition, 4-shaft Bedford cord fabric can have some stability problems, especially with slippery yarns, where the underlying floats can migrate to the right side of the fabric. But you can solve that problem with stitcher warps.

ADDING STITCHER WARPS

To keep the weft floats on the wrong side of the fabric, we add stitcher warps on shafts 5 and 6 (white warps) between each of the ribs, as shown in Figure 2. (These are referred to as cutting ends in some books.) The stitcher warps are *woven by every pick of weft*, creating a small section of plain weave between each rib. The stitchers stabilize the weft floats and add definition between the ribs **(see Figure 2)**.

To hide the stitcher warps, wind the stitcher warp threads to match the colors in the adjacent ribs. So the first stitcher (which is between the first orange stripe and the first blue stripe), threaded on shaft 5 on our draft, should be orange and the second stitcher warp, threaded on shaft 6, should be blue. Now we move to the first blue stripe. On the other side of the first blue stripe, the stitcher warp on shaft 5 will be blue , and the one on shaft 6, adjacent to the orange stripe, will be orange.

When you wind the warp, in the first rib there will be nine orange warp threads (eight warp threads for the orange rib plus an orange stitcher warp on shaft 5) followed by ten blue warp threads (one for the stitcher warp on shaft 6, eight warp threads for the blue rib, and 1 stitcher warp on shaft 5 for the next stitcher warp set), and then ten of each color until the last stripe. If the stitcher warps are of a contrasting color to the rib warps, a fine line of the contrasting color will show between each rib. This can be another fun design element.

ADDING SUPPLEMENTAL WARPS

You have undoubtedly noticed that to this point, Bedford cord doesn't use or need a supplemental warp. But this is a book about supplemental warps! Now we cross that threshold. To add definition to the ribs, we add supplemental wadding warps in each of the cord sections. The wadding adds padding and more definition to the ribs in your fabric.

IMPORTANT NOTE: For consistency in this example, I have been using the traditional shaft set up for Bedford cord. I will continue using the traditional shaft set up in this sample, but if you follow this draft, you will need to thread the supplemental warps at the same time as the fabric warp threads. The draft for the Bedford cord rug project has been flipped to utilize my technique of first threading all fabric warps then threading the supplemental warps. (See Chapters 1 and 2 for details and reasons to use this technique.) However, if you warp front to back, you won't need to flip the Bedford cord draft.

As you can see in Figure 3, one supplemental warp is threaded between each of the plain-weave picks in the rib sections. Note the tie-up: Supplemental warps for the ribs threaded on shafts 1 and 2 (block A) are always threaded on shaft 7. Supplemental warps for sections threaded on shafts 3 and 4 (block B) are always on shaft 8.

When weaving, the supplemental warps lay between the plain-weave top layer and the weft floats of the bottom layer. *The supplemental warps will never intersect with either side of the fabric,* and therefore they don't have any take-up. When winding supplemental warps, I usually recommend adding 10–12 inches to the supplemental warp length. With Bedford cord, there isn't take-up with the supplemental wadding warps, but because I like to have a little wiggle room, I advise adding 4 inches to the supplemental warp length. Remember, it's always better to have a little extra than to run short!

Now let's look Figure 3 to see how the supplemental warps work: Treadle 1 raises shaft 1 (to weave plain weave on top) plus shafts 3 and 4 (to get them out of the way so the weft floats under that section) and raises the

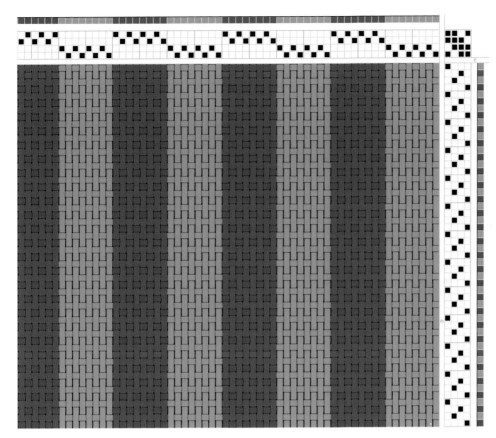

Figure 1. Bedford cord on 4 shafts

Stitcher warps

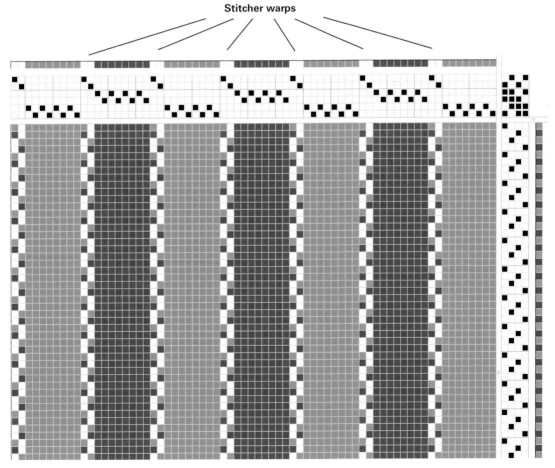

Figure 2. Bedford cord adding the stitching warps between sections

81

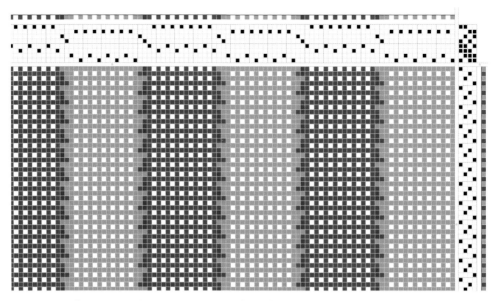

Figure 3. Bedford cord adding the supplemental wadding warps

all supplemental warps on shaft 8. Therefore, the weft *float* on the back of the fabric also encloses the supplemental warps in that entire rib section. Any supplemental warps on shaft 7 stay down and the weft interlaces above those supplemental warps. After the entire series of 4 picks, the supplemental warp in each block is snug inside a casing of weft floats on the back and plain weave on the top. The casing of weft floats attaches to the fabric at the stitcher warps on shafts 5 and 6 and keeps the supplemental wadding warps from moving between ribs.

Look closely at the drawdown shown here. You can see that the white supplemental warps never interlace with the orange and blue ribs on the top layer of the cloth. Computer drafting programs don't recognize that the supplemental warps are on the back of the fabric, so they are seen here as white dots showing through the cloth. In your weaving, the supplemental warps will be completely covered **(see Figure 3)**.

ONE LAST NOTE: To help control draw-in at the selvedges, you can add two stitcher warps on shafts 5 and 6 at the selvedges. These stitcher warps secure the weft float picks at the edges and reduce draw-in

Troubleshooting

Why are my supplemental warps weaving in with the top layers of the fabric?

If you have supplemental warps showing in the surface fabric, you have threaded them on the wrong shafts with the corresponding rib. It's all based on your tie-up.

Look closely at the first two ribs in Figure 4. In both these ribs, you can see the opposite weft color showing. Instead of interlacing with their own rib and floating on the back of the opposite rib, the rib weft color is interlacing with the supplemental warps and the weft that should be floating on the back of the fabric behind the supplemental warps is sandwiched between the fabric face and the supplemental warps. We need to rethread these two

stripes so that the supplemental warps for block A (shafts 1 and 2) are on shaft 7 and the supplemental warps for block B (shafts 3 and 4) are on shaft 8 **(see Figure 4)**.

How can I change a traditional Bedford cord draft so that the supplemental warps can be threaded after the fabric warps?

Chapter 1 has two easy ways to flip traditional Bedford cord drafts so you can thread all of the plain-weave warp threads and then all of the supplemental warp threads. As I mentioned earlier, if you warp back to front and use the traditional draft for Bedford cord, you must thread the supplemental warps (shafts 7 and 8) at the same time you thread the plain weave cord and stitcher shafts (shafts 1 through 6). If you try to thread all of the supplemental warps first on shafts 7 and 8, the supplemental warp threads will be in the way for attaching the regular warp to the apron rod. (Believe me, I tried it). If you try to thread all of the other warp threads first, you MUST move the heddles for shafts 7 and 8 into place while threading shafts 1-6, because the fabric warp threads will be in the way so you can't move the heddles into place.

It's easiest to just flip the draft to put the supplemental warp threads on shafts 1 and 2. As you can see in Figure 5, the rest of the draft just moves back two shafts: Block A is now on shafts 3 and 4, block B is on shafts 5 and 6, the stitcher threads are on shafts 7 and 8, and the supplemental warps for block A are on shaft 1 and for block B are in shaft 2. **(See Figure 5.)** Easy peasy!

Design Options for Bedford Cord

Bedford cord offers loads of options for playing with texture and color. You can change the width of the ribs across the fabric, either by alternating or by having different sequences of wide and narrow ribs. You can add wadding to some ribs and not others, or have different amounts of wadding in different ribs so they are thicker or thinner.

You can also play with color. Traditional Bedford cord

has the two weft colors alternating picks, so each rib is a solid color, but there are so many more possibilities.

If you wind all of your cloth warp in the same color and use the same color for weft, you will get solid color cloth defined by the texture of the ribs. You could have a narrow rib in a contrasting color in between wider ribs, or you could weave with two colors of weft in some or all of the blocks to get color blends. You could create selvedge-to-selvedge stripes by weaving with one color in both blocks. The patterns and combinations you can create are almost endless. Play!

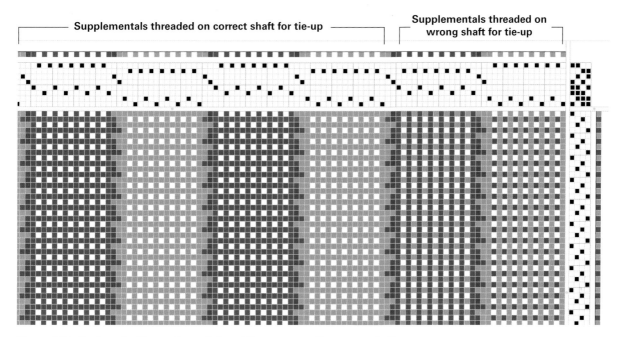

Figure 4. Bedford cord with supplemental wadding warps on the wrong shaft

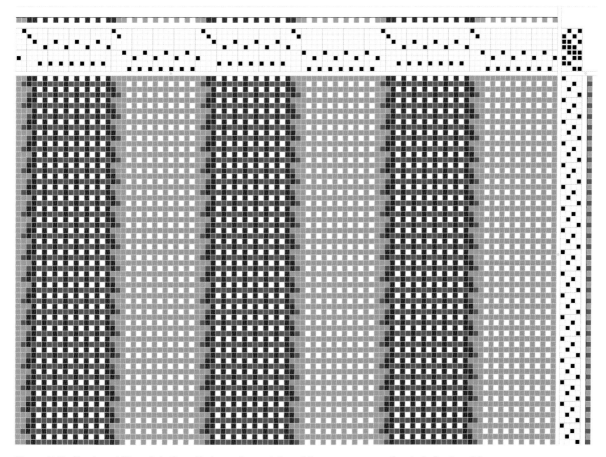

Figure 5. Bedford cord flipped draft so that supplemental wadding warps are on front shafts 1 and 2

Bedford Cord-Sometimes things don't go as planned

©iStockphoto.com/alessandro0770

Athena was the Greek goddess of weaving. I like to think she is still watching over all weavers as we continue to carry forward this ancient craft. After 20 years practicing the art of weaving, most of my projects go as planned. Note that I say "most". Regardless of what experienced weavers say and beginning weavers believe, things don't always go smoothly. When things are going well, I picture Athena smiling. When things aren't going right, I joke that Athena is tapping me on the shoulder trying to get my attention before things go completely off the rails. She's that little voice in my head saying, "Something's not quite right here." Usually I pay attention and catch the errors quickly. If I ignore her, things generally go from bad to worse. The Bedford cord project for this book was one of those times

The Bedford cord project started like all others. I designed the rug, decided on the yarn and colors, and calculated the amount of yarn I needed. That's when things started to veer off track. I called our local yarn shop owner to see what colors she still had left in the Jason Collingwood rug wools. The owner informed me that she had recently sold all of the stock! However, she had a bunch of Harrisville Highland wool yarn, and it was on sale! I took that as a "sign" and purchased two cones, one in Navy Blue and one in Garnet.

Mistake #1

Before going to the shop, I looked at the Harrisville website and saw the notation "900 yards per pound" for Highland yarn. What I neglected to notice was that Harrisville Highland wool is sold on 8-ounce cones, so each cone held only 450 yards. Oblivious to my error, I wound the two warps. I had just barely enough of the Garnet for the contrast stripes and the supplemental warps and not enough on the Navy Blue to weave the entire rug. I then had to wait three days for the shop to open for their Wednesday–Saturday hours, and I rejoiced that there still was another cone of Navy Blue in the shop. Whew!

Mistakes #2, 3, and 4

I always thread the ground warp first and supplemental warp second. This requires the supplemental warps to be on the front shafts. However, on this project I had the "brilliant" idea of threading the supplemental warp first on the back shafts (per the original draft) and pulling the ground cloth warps through the supplemental warps. Athena tapped me on the shoulder and said, "Are you sure about this?"

But I ignored her and plunged ahead. After threading all of the supplemental warps, I realized the supplemental warp would be under the ground cloth warp and, instead of hanging freely as they need to do, they would be trapped between the ground cloth warp and the back beam. Unwilling to lose all the time spent threading, I spent another 20 minutes muttering, re-arranging, and trying to figure out how to make it work. Finally, I admitted defeat and pulled the supplemental warp ends out of the heddles. This is when Athena started tapping me on the shoulder again. But I was in a rush and angry about the wasted time, and I ignored her.

Then I threaded all of the ground cloth warp ends on the front shafts. . . forgetting to move heddles for the supplemental warp on the back shafts. You can't move heddles on the back shafts past a warp that is already threaded on the front shafts, so I pulled everything out again. At this point, Athena gave me a hard shove, and I took the time to flip my draft (which I should have done in the first place), and threaded the warps.

Mistake #5

I completely missed threading one thread of the supplemental warps. Easy fix: Make a string heddle.

Mistake #6

By now I had the draft memorized, so I didn't even take it to the loom. As I was threading, I got in my head that the supplemental warp threads on Shaft 1 went with the ground warps on shafts 3 and 4, and the supplemental warp threads on Shaft 2 went with shafts 1 and 2. All of which is the opposite of how it was supposed to be, so the supplemental warps were weaving in with the regular warp instead of floating between the layers. Quick fix: Change the tie-up. I'm sure Athena was laughing by now.

The last insult to my injury was a broken selvedge thread halfway thru the weaving. Lesson: Add a set of stitcher warps on each of the selvedge edges to anchor the floating weft picks and help control the draw-in.

I'm sharing this story because if I hadn't made all of these mistakes, I probably wouldn't have included as many warnings and information on how to fix mistakes in this book. All in all, things worked out in the end. Perhaps, that was Athena's plan all along.

Project at a Glance:
Bedford Cord Rug

STRUCTURE
Bedford cord.

EQUIPMENT
8-shaft loom, 32" weaving width; 8-dent reed; 1 shuttle with bobbin.

YARNS
Background warp: 100% wool, worsted weight (900 yd/lb; Harrisville Highland), Navy Blue, 364 yd; Garnet, 140 yd.
Supplemental warp: wool, worsted weight, Garnet, 364 yd.
Weft: wool, worsted weight, Navy Blue, 308 yd.

WARP LENGTH
Background warp: 252 ends 2 yd long (allows 6" for take-up, 26" for loom waste). **Supplemental warp:** 49 ends 2¼ yd long (23 sections of 7 ends each).

SETTS
Warp: 8 epi (1/dent in an 8-dent reed). In supplemental warp sections, sley 1 background warp plus 1 supplemental warp end per dent.
Weft: 8 ppi.

DIMENSIONS
Width in the reed: 31½".
Woven length (measured under tension on the loom): 40".
Finished size: 22½" x 35".

STEP BY STEP INSTRUCTIONS

Step 1   Wind 248 warp threads 2 yd long of the background warp, following the warp color order in Figure 6. Wind 23 separate supplemental warp chains of the Garnet 21/4 yd long, 7 threads in each bout. Set the supplemental warp bouts aside. Thread the background warps according to the directions in Chapter 2, following the draft in Figure 7. (Note that the warp ends on shafts 7 and 8 are the stitcher warps.)

Step 2   Lay supplemental warps on the loom as described in Chapter 2. Count 10r warps from the first selvedge, bundle and push them aside, and begin thread the supplemental warp threads according to the draft, Figure 7. (To help the rug lie flat, there is no wadding in the first section at each edge.) As you finish threading each section, bundle the supplemental warps with the background warps (including the stitcher warps), and push aside. Continue until all the supplemental warp sections are threaded. You should have 12 background warp ends left to the selvedge.

Step 3   Sley the reed, centering for a 31½" weaving width. There will be 1 end/dent in the background-only areas. The supplemental warp sections will have 1 background warp end and 1 supplemental warp end per dent.

Step 4   Tie on as you normally would, allowing for 4" of fringe. Work in small sections of warp. This warp is very bulky, so the lashing method works very well for tie-on to the front apron rod. Weight the supplemental warp bouts over the back beam. Adjust your background warp tension to match that provided by the weights.

Step 5   Before you start weaving the rug, create a header for your weaving by twining around the warp threads in groups of 4 dents worth of yarn, using a 3-yd length of blue yarn. (With this thick yarn, there is too much bulk to do overhand knots in the fringe, so we use twining to secure of the warp ends. See inset Single-Color Twining.)

Step 6   Wind a bobbin of weft yarn. Weave 40" following the treadling repeat in the draft, then use twining to finish the end.

Step 7   Machine zig-zag across both ends to secure wefts and warps. Remove all scrap yarns.

Step 8   Handwash in warm water (a bathtub works great) and lay flat to dry. For regular cleaning, the rug can be washed in a machine on the handwash cycle, then laid flat to dry

Figure 7. Draft

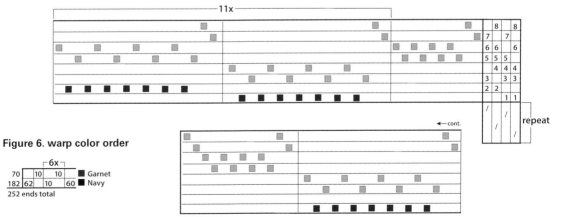

Figure 6. warp color order

	┌6x┐				
70	10	10		▣	Garnet
182	62	10	60	■	Navy
252 ends total					

▣ background warp
(wind according to Figure 1, warp color order; beam and thread first)
■ supplemental warp
(do not beam; thread separately)

Piqué – Fabric That Goes Poof!

LIKE BEDFORD CORD, PIQUÉ TAKES FABRIC into three dimensions. Bedford cord uses supplemental warps (wadding) to raise the right (top) side of the fabric up into ribs that run the length of the fabric. Piqué uses supplemental warps (stitchers) to secure supplemental *wefts* (stuffers) that float on the back of the fabric, creating ribs from selvedge to selvedge. The stitcher warps also rise to the surface to interlace with the plain-weave face cloth and create pattern.

Like Bedford cord, piqué is a one sided fabric. The wrong side of the fabric shows the stuffer picks, so this fabric is useful for projects where only the right side of the fabric shows, such as upholstery or pillow covers, or it can be sewn to a backing fabric and used for throws, blankets, shawls, or clothing.

Choosing Yarns

You can use any smooth yarn you like for the plain-weave fabric. The supplemental stitcher warps work best if you use yarns such as cotton and wool, that have a little elasticity, but I've had success with silk, bamboo and Tencel as well. Linen would not be a good choice for this purpose.

Stuffer wefts should be a color similar to your plain-weave fabric so the stuffer weft doesn't peek through. Large wool yarns make the best stuffer wefts. My stash of wool mill ends is used often for this purpose. The more or the thicker stuffer yarns you use, the more prominent will be the ribs in your fabric. Because the stuffing is added as the fabric is woven, you can vary your treadling and change the number or size of the stuffer weft yarns to create larger or smaller ribs. Just insert the stuffer weft picks halfway between the picks where the stitcher warps interlace with the plain-weave cloth. (For example, if you're weaving a rib ½ inch wide, insert the stuffer weft pick at the ¼-inch point.) As a rule of thumb, there should be 1 inch or less of woven surface fabric between supplemental warp stitcher picks to maximize the "poof" of the piqué.

The supplemental warps need to be woven under high tension, so they need more weight on them than most types of supplemental warps. When the fabric is removed from the loom, the stretched supplemental warps return to their original lengths and the take-up on the stitchers works with the stuffer wefts to pull the ground cloth into ribs.

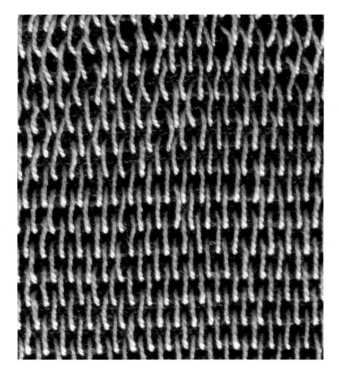

Photo 1. Back view of loose-back piqué

Photo 2. Back view of fast-back piqué

Piqué fabric must be wet-finished to achieve the full "poof" effect of the design. Test all yarns—stuffer wefts, supplemental warps, and plain-weave fabric yarns—for bleeding by washing a small amount of each yarn separately and then check for any dye in the water. If there is any bleeding you don't want to use that yarn. How awful to weave a beautiful piqué piece only to have it blotched with dye during the wet-finishing.

Fast-Back vs Loose-Back Piqué

There are two ways to weave piqué: fast back and loose back. The difference is in the interlacement of the supplemental stitcher warps with the stuffer wefts.

In loose-back piqué, the stuffer wefts are sandwiched between the plain-weave fabric and the supplemental warp floats on the wrong side of the fabric. They never interlace with the stitcher warps or the plain-weave cloth. Basic loose-back piqué requires only three shafts: two for the plain-weave fabric and one for the supplemental warp. The stuffer weft is placed by raising both plain-weave shafts and leaving the supplemental warps down **(see Photo 1)**.

In fast-back piqué, the stuffer weft interlaces with the stitcher warps in an over/under, plain-weave sequence on the wrong side of the fabric. Fast-back piqué requires at least four shafts to weave: two for the plain-weave face cloth and two to weave the stuffer wefts with the supplemental warp. As you weave the stuffer picks, you alternate raising the supplemental stitcher warps together with both surface fabric shafts so that the stuffer wefts weave over and under the supplemental stitcher warps **(see Photo 2)**.

Both fabrics look the same from the front side, but fast-back piqué is much more stable if you are planning to cut the fabric. Cutting loose-back piqué can release the tension on the supplemental warps and lose some of the "poof".

Comparing Piqué Drafts

Let's look a bit closer at these two piqué structures. (Remember that the drafts in this book use my threading technique, with the plain-weave warps on the back shafts and the supplemental warps on the front shafts, so they will look different than traditional drafts in other books. To change traditional piqué drafts to my threading technique, refer to Chapter 3.)

Loose-back piqué

The draft shown in Figure 1 is for loose-back piqué. At first glance, the threading looks like plain weave at the selvedges, interrupted periodically by a 3-shaft straight twill threading. But look closely at the tie-up. Treadles 1 and 2 are direct tie-up to shafts 2 and 3. These two treadles are weaving the plain-weave surface cloth, while shaft 1 lies neutral, causing the stitcher warp to float on the back of the fabric. Shaft 1 lifts the supplemental stitcher warps, which are orange on the draft. Treadles 3 and 4 are used to engage the stitcher warps: they lift shafts 2 and 3, respectively, plus shaft 1, making the supplemental stitcher warps float on the surface of the fabric.

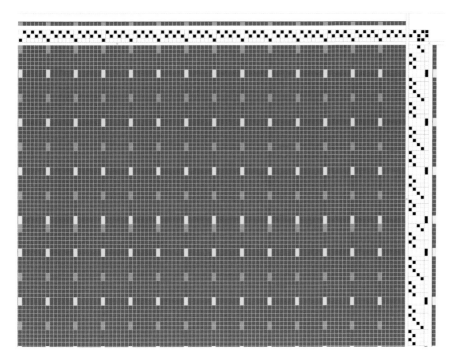

Figure 1. Example of loose-back piqué draft

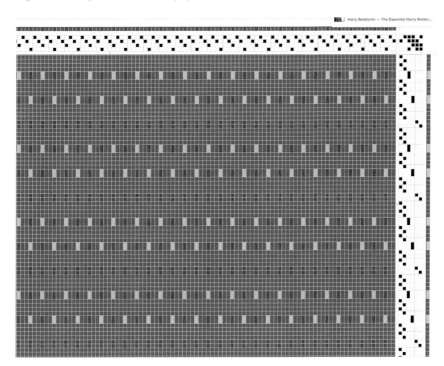

Figure 2. Example of fast-back piqué draft

When Treadle 5 is pressed, both plain-weave shafts are raised and the supplemental stitcher warp stays down, leaving a channel for a pick of supplemental stuffer weft (wider, yellow spots in the drawdown, but remember that the stuffer will not show in the real cloth.)

Note that the stuffer wefts catch and turn where the stitcher warps start. If you want the "poof" created by the stuffer yarns to run from selvedge to selvedge, you need to place stitcher supplemental warps close to the selvedge edge. In the piqué projects, one pillow cover has the stuffer wefts running the width of the cloth. One pillow cover has the stuffers only in the middle sections where the supplemental warps are threaded.

Fast-back Piqué

Now let's look at a draft for fast-back piqué, **Figure 2**. Once again, the plain-weave surface cloth warps are threaded on the back shafts, in this draft, the blue threads on shafts 3 and 4, which are direct-tied to treadles 1 and 2. The supplemental stitcher warps are the red warp ends threaded on shafts 1 and 2.

There are two wadding picks (wider green weft) in the treadling between each pick where supplemental stitchers interlace with the plain-weave face cloth. Note that while a red supplemental warp raises in the stuffer warp picks, the red supplemental warp threads *do not interlace* with the plain-weave threads.

Treadle 3 raises both surface fabric shafts (3 and 4) plus the shaft 1 stitcher warps, and treadle 4 raises both surface fabric shafts plus the shaft 2 stitcher warps . When treadles 3 and 4 are raised in succession, the stuffer weft passes under the surface fabric shafts and weaves plain weave with the stitcher warps.

Look closely at the drawdown. In contrast to the loose-back piqué, where only the green stuffer warp shows across the fabric on a stuffer pick, in the fast-back draft, the colors alternate green (stuffer) and red (supplemental warp), and the colors shift on the two stuffer picks in each set, showing the plain-weave structure of the interlacement. The final stitcher picks for the sequence come *after both* stuffer picks.

For this draft, there are two sets of surface fabric picks between the stuffer picks. You can weave two, four, or more surface picks between the stuffer picks, and the "poof" of the rib will depend on the thickness and number of yarns you use for stuffer weft. **(See Photo 3.)** The only rule is that there must be an even number of surface fabric picks between stuffer picks to maintain the integrity of the fabric interlacing with the stitcher

Photo 3. Contrast between single stuffer and multiple stuffer wefts

warps. How do you know how much to weave between stuffer picks? Sample, sample, sample.

More Design Possibilities

Piqué has many design possibilities beyond just straight ribs across the fabric. If you have enough shafts available, you can use twill threadings for the supplemental stitcher warps to create waves or diamonds across the fabric. You still need 2 shafts devoted to the plain-weave surface fabric. The number of pattern shafts you'll need depends on the twill design you choose, and the number of treadles will depend on whether you're doing loose-back or fast-back piqué. So say you choose a four-shaft point twill pattern. You'll need two shafts for the plain-weave surface fabric plus four shafts for the stitcher pattern, for a total of six shafts. If you're weaving loose-back piqué, you'll need two treadles for the plain-weave surface fabric picks while leaving the stitcher warps down, one treadle to lift both surface fabric shafts while leaving the stitcher warps down for a stuffer weft pick, and four treadles to lift stitcher warps with one or the other surface fabric shaft to create the stitcher pattern. If you want a fast-back piqué in twill, you will need the same number of shafts, but more treadles tied up so the wadding picks alternate with the stitcher warps across the wrong side of the fabric. A direct tie-up on a jack loom cuts down on the number of treadles needed, because you can press two treadles at the same time to achieve the interlacement of the stitcher warps and the stuffer weft. If you have a countermarch loom, you may be restricted because each shaft combination must have its own treadle.

The pillow project section has the draft for waved piqué with a point-twill pattern in the supplemental stitcher warps. Here's a draft for diamond piqué to play with on your own. Note that this draft utilizes a direct tie-up for treadles, so two treadles need to be pressed at the same time in the supplemental warp pattern picks. The orange weft picks are the stuffer picks; you need to use a large weavers angle for your stuffer weft picks so there is enough stuffer weft to travel around the designs. This is necessary whether weaving fast back or loose back piqué. The stuffer wefts are going around the points of the diamond twill design and you need enough stuffer weft to travel over those points to avoiding excessive draw-in of the plain weave fabric from the stuffer wefts pulling in on the selvedges as they make the journey across the diamond points. Photo 6-3 shows this draft with and without stuffer wefts and you can see how the stuffer wefts travel over the points. The bottom point of the next diamond shape will push the stuffer wefts down, the top points push the stuffer wefts up **(see Figure 3)**.

See Chapter 3 to learn how to convert this draft so that the plain-weave surface cloth is on the back shafts. This is how the draft will look after moving the surface-fabric threads to the back shafts **(see Figure 4)**.

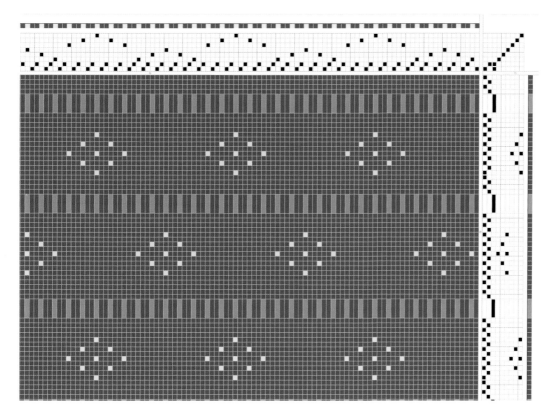

Figure 3. Figured loose-back piqué draft with supplemental warps on back shafts

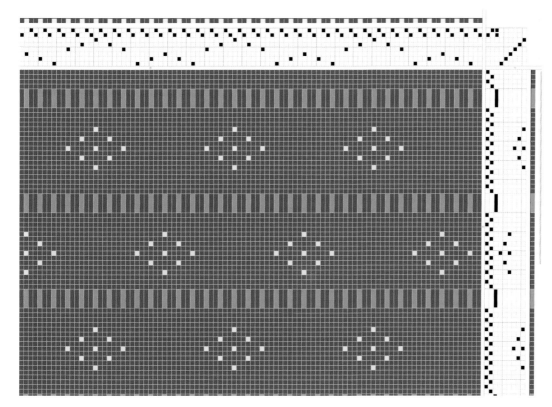

Figure 4. Figured loose-back piqué draft with supplemental warps on front shafts

Project at a Glance: Ribbed Piqué Pillow

STRUCTURE
Loose-back piqué.

EQUIPMENT
4-shaft loom, 20" weaving width; 10-dent reed; 2 shuttles with bobbins.

YARNS
Ground warp: 10/2 pearl cotton (4,200 yd/lb), dark blue, 900 yd.
Supplemental warp: 10/2 pearl cotton, gold, 160 yd.
Ground weft: 10/2 pearl cotton, navy blue, 538 yd.
Stuffer weft: Wool rug or knitting yarn, DK to bulky weight, 25 yd.
(I used **WEBS Valley Cotton Line:** 10/2 pearl cotton, #2655 Victoria Blue and #7129 Golden Ochre.)

OTHER SUPPLIES
16" pillow form; sewing thread; decorative trim, 2 yd.

Warp Length: Background warp: 400 ends 2¼ yd (allows 5" for take-up, 32" for sampling and loom waste). **Supplemental warp:** 64 ends (4 sections of 12 ends each and 1 section of 16 ends) 2½ yd long.

SETTS
Warp: 20 epi (2/dent in a 10-dent reed) for background cloth. Sley 1 supplemental warp with 2 background warps (3/dent). **Weft:** 20 ppi.

DIMENSIONS
Width in the reed: 20". Woven length (measured under tension on the loom): 44". Finished size after washing: 1 pillow, 16" x 16".

STEP BY STEP INSTRUCTIONS

Step 1 Wind 400 warp threads 2¼ yd long of the background warp. Wind 5 supplemental warp chains 2½ yd long, 4 of 12 ends and 1 of 16 ends. Thread the background warps according to the directions in Chapter 2, following the draft in Figure 1, and tie with slipknots in groups of 6.

Step 2 Lay supplemental warps on the loom as described in Chapter 2. Thread the supplemental warps on shaft 1, one supplemental warp between each group of 6 background warps, as shown in the draft.

Step 3 Sley the reed, centering for a 20" weaving width. There will be 2 ends/dent except where there are supplemental warp threads, which will be sleyed with 2 background warps.

Step 4 Tie on using your preferred method, including the pattern warps with the background warp in the tie-on groups. Weight the supplemental warp bouts over the back beam. You need strong tension on these supplemental warps, so more weight is better.

Step 5 Wind a bobbin of background weft yarn and one of the stuffer weft. To spread the warps and anchor the supplemental warps, weave a couple of inches with waste yarn, treadling 1, 2, 3, 4. Weave 1" of plain weave for hem. Weave piqué sequence twice, as shown in Figure 5, then weave 1" of plain weave. To help hold the supplemental warps taught until sewn, finish by weaving about 1" with waste yarn or rags, treadling 1, 2, 3, 4.

Step 6 Cut fabric off loom and machine zig-zag the ends.

Step 7 Handwash in warm water and lay flat to dry.

Sewing

Note: Because cutting the fabric will set the supplemental warps "free", do not cut the fabric to size first.

Step 1 Fold the fabric, in half right sides together, so that the two middle sections with narrower space (4 picks total) between stitchers line up

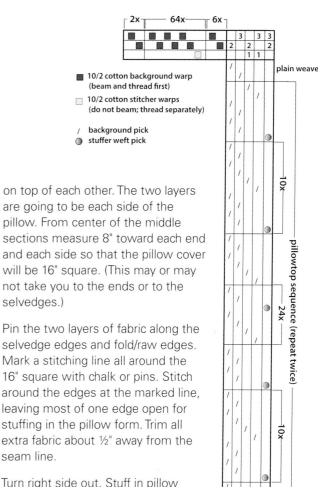

Figure 5. Ribbed Piqué draft

■ 10/2 cotton background warp (beam and thread first)
□ 10/2 cotton stitcher warps (do not beam; thread separately)
/ background pick
● stuffer weft pick

on top of each other. The two layers are going to be each side of the pillow. From center of the middle sections measure 8" toward each end and each side so that the pillow cover will be 16" square. (This may or may not take you to the ends or to the selvedges.)

Step 2 Pin the two layers of fabric along the selvedge edges and fold/raw edges. Mark a stitching line all around the 16" square with chalk or pins. Stitch around the edges at the marked line, leaving most of one edge open for stuffing in the pillow form. Trim all extra fabric about ½" away from the seam line.

Step 3 Turn right side out. Stuff in pillow form, turn edges of opening in and handstitch closed.

If you decide to add the decorative trim, you will need to cut the fabric before stitching the seams around all of the edges. In that case, mark the 16" square and then individually machine stitch each layer of fabric ¼" away from that line (toward what will be the seam) all the way around the pillow. Trim excess fabric to the same width as the seam allowance on the decorative trim. (The seam allowance on decorative trims varies, so be sure to measure.) Pin and then baste the trim to the seam line on the right side of one piece of fabric so the decorative part is flat against the fabric and away from the raw edge of the fabric. Pin the two pieces of fabric together so the edges meet, then use a zipper presser foot to stitch as close as possible to the decorative trim all the way around 3 edges, leaving enough room on the last edge to insert the pillow form.

Project at a Glance: Waved Piqué Pillow

STRUCTURE
Loose-back piqué.

EQUIPMENT
6-shaft loom, 20" weaving width; 10-dent reed; 2 shuttles with bobbins.

YARNS
Ground warp: 10/2 pearl cotton (4,200 yd/lb), gold, 800 yd.
Supplemental warp: 10/2 pearl cotton, navy blue, 142 yd.
Ground weft: 10/2 pearl cotton, gold, 490 yd.
Stuffer weft: Wool rug or knitting yarn, DK to bulky weight, 118 yd. (Choose a yarn that is relatively lofty and soft, to bend around the angles in the pattern.)

(I used WEBS Valley Cotton Line: 10/2 pearl cotton, #2655 Victoria Blue and #7129 Golden Ochre.)

OTHER SUPPLIES
16" pillow form; sewing thread; decorative trim, 2 yd.

Warp Length: Background warp: 400 ends 2 yd (allows 5" for take-up, 27" for sampling and loom waste).
Supplemental warp: 63 ends (3 sections of 21 ends each) 2¼ yd long.

SETTS
Warp: 20 epi (2/dent in a 10-dent reed) for background cloth. In supplemental warp areas, sley 1 supplemental warp with 2 background warps (3/dent).
Weft: 20 ppi (ground cloth).

DIMENSIONS
Width in the reed: 20".
Woven length (measured under tension on the loom): 40".
Finished size after washing: 1 pillow, 16" x 16".

STEP BY STEP INSTRUCTIONS

Step 1 — Wind 400 warp threads 2 yd long of the background warp. Wind 3 supplemental warp chains 2¼ yd long, 40 ends each. Thread the background warps according to the directions in Chapter 2, following the draft in Figure 2, and tie with slipknots in groups of 4 for easy counting.

Step 2 — Lay supplemental warps on the loom as described in Chapter 2. Start threading the supplemental warps 4" (80 background warp ends) from the edge, as shown in the draft. The supplemental warps are threaded with one supplemental warp between 2 background warps.

Step 3 — Sley the reed, centering for a 20" weaving width. There will be 2 ends/dent in plain weave sections and 3 ends/dent in supplemental warp sections.

Step 4 — Tie on using your preferred method, including the pattern warps with the background warp in the tie-on groups. Weight the supplemental warp bouts over the back beam. You need strong tension on these supplemental warps, so more weight is better.

Step 5 — Wind a bobbin of background weft yarn and one of the stuffer weft. To spread the warps and anchor the supplemental warps, weave a couple of inches with waste yarn, treadling 1, 2, 3, 4. Weave 1" of plain weave for hem. Weave piqué for 38", as shown in Figure 1, then weave 1" of plain weave. Remember to use a large weavers angle for your stuffer weft picks so there is enough stuffer weft to travel around the designs. To help hold the supplemental warps taught until sewn, finish by weaving about 1" with waste yarn or rags, treadling 1, 2, 3, 4.

Step 6 — Cut fabric off loom and machine zig-zag the ends.

Step 7 — Handwash in warm water and lay flat to dry.

Sewing

Note: Because cutting the fabric will set the supplemental warps "free", do not cut the fabric to size first.

Step 1 — Fold the fabric, in half right sides together. Measure a 16" square. (This may or may not take you to the ends or to the selvedges.)

Step 2 — Pin the two layers of fabric along the selvedge edges and fold/raw edges. Mark a stitching line all around the 16" square with chalk or pins. Stitch around the edges at the marked line, leaving most of one edge open for stuffing in the pillow form. Trim all extra fabric about ½" away from the seam line.

Step 3 — Turn right side out. Stuff in pillow form, turn edges of opening in, and handstitch closed.

If you decide to add the decorative trim, you will need to cut the fabric before stitching the seams around all of the edges. In that case, mark the 16" square and then individually machine stitch each layer of fabric ¼" away from that line (toward what will be the seam) all the way around the pillow. Trim excess fabric to the same width as the seam allowance on the decorative trim. (The seam allowance on decorative trims varies, so be sure to measure.) Pin and then baste the trim to the seam line on the right side of one piece of fabric so the decorative part is flat against the fabric and away from the raw edge of the fabric. Pin the two pieces of fabric together so the edges meet, then use a zipper presser foot to stitch as close as possible to the decorative trim all the way around 3 edges, leaving enough room on the last edge to insert the pillow form.

Figure 5. Waved Piqué Draft

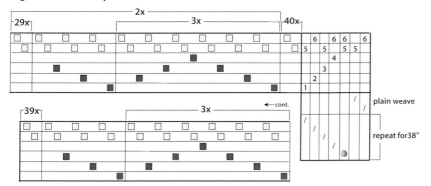

□ 10/2 cotton background warp
(beam and thread first)

■ 10/2 cotton stitcher warps
(do not beam; thread separately)

/ background pick
● stuffer weft pick

plain weave

repeat for 38"

Terry-Cloth Towels

THE "TERRY" IN TERRY-CLOTH comes from the French word *tirer*, which means "to pull out." Weaving terry-cloth involves a plain-weave ground cloth with a supplemental warp that is pulled up into loops, creating pile, typically on both sides of the cloth. Research by The Textile Institute in Manchester, United Kingdom, indicates that the technique originated in Turkey and was likely a result of a mistake! However, weavers being resourceful folks, the Turks discovered that the loops made a more absorbent towel, and a "mistake" became a weaving innovation.

The loops in terry-cloth are created by inserting a rod under supplemental warp threads, then adding plain-weave picks to secure the loops before the rods are removed. (We will use wooden dowels for rods.) True terry-cloth has uncut loops, but you can choose to cut the loops to make pile, as is done in many commercial towels. If the loops are cut, the fabric becomes *velour*, derived *vellus*, the Latin word for hair. Typically, velour is a one-sided fabric, but there can be loops on the back and cut loops on the front. Velour towels are more absorbent, but don't hold up as well with regular use as the looped pile in terry-cloth towels.

Industry standards dictate that there are five basic parts to a towel: Selvedges, fringe (optional), beginning and ending plain-weave sections (to anchor the supplemental warps for the loops), the pile sections, and borders (plain-weave sections within the pile section). Loops can be drawn up on both sides of the fabric or just one side (typically the top of the fabric).

Terry-cloth weaving works best with suspended and weighted supplemental warps rather than using a second warp beam. The loops take up so much yarn with each pick that if you use a second beam, you will be advancing the pile warp constantly, whereas a weighted warp can just feed smoothly forward as you need it.

Selecting Yarns

Weaving terry-cloth towels is slow, but the resulting fabric is so soft and absorbent, you may be tempted to replace all your machine-made towels! One supplemental warp for the pile is threaded between each pair of ground warp ends, making a 2:1 ratio. The number of plain-weave picks between the pile picks determines the density of the towel. The fewer ground cloth picks, the closer we can pack together the pile rows and the denser the pile. Commercially made towels usually have two or three picks of plain weave between pile picks. The plain-weave picks lock the pile picks into the ground cloth, so *you* must have at least two, but you can choose have up to seven picks of ground cloth between pile picks. When you see reference to 3-pick terry, this refers to two picks of plain weave plus one pile pick.

Terry-cloth is typically woven with cotton yarns. Cotton is soft, widely available, inexpensive, absorbent, dyes well, becomes stronger when wet, returns to its original shape after wetting, and typically does not cause an allergic reaction. Also, cotton yarn has better elasticity than other plant fibers and is therefore easier to pull up evenly into pile loops.

Cotton is the industry standard for terry-cloth towels, but that doesn't mean you have to use it. Linen, cottolin (a blend of cotton and linen), and bamboo all make wonderful towels. Linen pile doesn't feel as soft as cotton or cottolin pile loops, and linen can be tricky to work with as the supplemental pile warp, so it might not be the best yarn for your first terry-cloth project. However, linen makes wonderful, long lasting towels that are very absorbent.

Machine-made towels typically use 20/2 or 24/2 cotton for the ground cloth. However, for the handweaver, 10/2 cotton works very well and is readily available. Mercerized or unmercerized cotton work equally well. I like using mercerized cotton for the ground cloth warp and weft for strength and unmercerized cotton in supplemental warp pile loops for softness and absorbency.

A rule of thumb is to select a pile yarn that is one size larger than the yarn used for the ground cloth. For example, if you use a 10/2 ground cloth yarn, choose an 8/2 pile warp yarn. Machine-made towels typically use a 16/1 or 20/1 pile warp. Single-ply yarns like these have better absorbency and are softer on the skin than a 2-ply yarn, however they are harder for handweavers to find and easier to break in the supplemental warp. Typically, unless you use a very tightly twisted 2-ply yarn, you will probably not notice the difference between 2-ply or 1-ply yarns in the pile loops.

For terry-cloth, the ground warp sett should be less than you would typically use based on wraps per inch. For example, 10/2 mercerized cotton wraps to 40 ends per inch (wpi). When you divide by 2 (the calculation for plain weave), you get a sett of 20 epi. But remember that in terry-cloth, the pile warps are woven into the plain-weave ground cloth between every two ground warp threads, so the total sett would be 30 epi. With such a dense sett, it is difficult to beat the pile picks close together. Using a plain-weave sett of 16 or 18 epi gives the yarns room to move.

To more accurately calculate your sett, hold one ground warp yarn and one pile warp yarn next to each other and wrap them around a ruler for one inch as if they were one thread being careful not to twist the yarns together when you wrap the yarns. To avoid twisting them, hold the yarns close together and turn the ruler instead of winding the yarns around the ruler. Count the number of wraps of both yarns (one ground warp/one pile warp) as if they were one yarn, then divide by 2. This will give you the combined sett for both yarns.

For the project in this chapter, the wrap test yields 32 combined wraps per inch for a ground warp sett of 16 epi.

Calculating Warp Length and Winding the Warps

For terry-cloth, calculate the ground warp length the same as you would for any plain-weave cloth. (See Chapter 4 or the appendix for formulas to calculate your ground cloth warp.) The *supplemental* warps need to be long enough to create all the rows of loops in the towel. We will use dowels to create loops. Depending on the size of the dowels you use, the supplemental pile warps will need to be 2 to 4 times longer than the ground warp, which is a pretty wide range. As someone who doesn't like to waste yarn, I have come up with the following calculation for determining the *weaving length* of the supplemental warps:

> **(woven project length including hems x (circumference of dowel x # of pile picks per inch)) + (woven project length × .1 for plain-weave take-up) = weaving length for each supplemental warp.**

Once you have the weaving length, then you just have to add enough extra length for loom waste. As a general rule, I find that doubling my usual loom waste allowance is sufficient. Note that we are calculating take-up only on the *woven* length of the project, not on the *total* length of the supplemental warps, because there is minimal take-up in the plain weave picks between loop picks, and the formula is calculating the amount needed to create all the rows of loops.

Let's walk through this calculation for our towel project. We've decided to weave a set of two towels, each measuring 24" of terry-cloth weaving plus hem allowance of 2" on each end for a woven length of 28" per towel. The total woven length is 28" per towel × 2 = 56".

To measure the circumference of your dowel, wrap a small piece of paper around the dowel, starting at one end of the paper, and mark where the paper overlaps the end. Unroll the paper and measure from the end to the mark you made. Dowels are sold by diameter, so when I measure around a ³⁄₁₆" dowel, the circumference is approximately ⅝". To simplify the math, let's round up to ¾" circumference. Remember, it's always better to have a little more length than to run short at the end.

A balanced plain weave sett at 16 epi also has 16 picks per inch (ppi), but terry-cloth includes both ground and pile picks. For every 2 plain-weave picks in our project, we will have 1 pile pick—a 2:1 ratio. So for every 16 plain-weave picks, there are 8 pile picks—4 on the top of the cloth and 4 on the bottom— for a combined weft density of 24 ppi. (24 ppi is possible because we are using a looser than average sett for the 10/2 cotton yarn.)

We are planning to weave a total of 56" of towels. So here is the formula filled in:

(56" woven length × (¾" dowel circumference × 8 pile picks per inch)) + (56" woven length × .1) = 341.6" weaving length of supplemental warp needed.

So let's round up to 342", and now we have to add enough length for loom waste and a woven header. On my countermarch loom, the loom (thrum) waste allowance is 18" but I've found that 30" of loom waste plus an allowance for tie-on and a header is enough length to drape and weight the supplemental warps over the back apron rod as you get to the end of your warp. I tie-on to the apron rod using the lashing method, so all I need to add for the header is enough to weave with waste yarn to even out the warp threads. If you tie your warp threads directly to the apron rod, be sure to add that length on as well. So:

342" weaving length + 3" header + 30" loom waste = 375" supplemental warp length

Now let's calculate the number of supplemental warp threads needed. One supplemental warp thread is threaded between every 2 ground warps, thus your sett for the supplemental warps is 8 epi. The pile loop sections are 16" wide. Total number of warp ends is 8 epi × 16" = 128 supplemental warp ends.

Avoiding the Concorde Fallacy

We've all been there. We plan a project; everything is purchased and ready to go. Then things start falling apart: threading mistakes, measuring mistakes, broken threads, yarns don't work well together, etc. Starting over would waste all of the time and money we've already put into the project, so we keep throwing more time and money into trying to fix the problems. In the end, we achieve either expensive success or expensive failure.

Years ago, I dyed a large hank of cotton chenille yarn for a project and in the dyeing process the hank became hopelessly snarled. I spent hours trying to untangle the mess to "save" that yarn. I couldn't waste all that time and money already spent! The more I worked, the worse the mess became until I finally hurled the snarled mass of yarn across the room in frustration. I would have been better off had I not even tried to untangle the mess and instead just started over with a new batch of yarn.

I was a victim of the Concorde fallacy: the false rationale that so much time, energy, and/or money has already been expended on a project that it is justifiable to spend exponentially more time, energy, and/or money to fix it. The term was invented by biologists studying wasp behavior, who found that the amount of energy that wasps expended in protecting a nest is greater than the amount of energy expended in building the nest in the first place. The name comes from the Concorde supersonic passenger jet, famous partly because the costs of building, flying, and maintaining the jet were not justified by the returns in ticket sales. Policymakers had invested lots of taxpayer money into developing the Concorde, and then attempted save the project by throwing more taxpayer money at it so they would not be accused of wasting the money already spent.

It's important to get past this "too big to fail" mentality. The key is recognizing when to keep working/correcting a project and when to cut it loose and start over. Sometimes, it's a hard decision.

Photo 1. Tensioning system for the pile warp

too dense to allow the pile rows to beat tightly together! My options were: 1) Re-thread and re-sley, removing all the extra supplemental warp yarns in the process, thus wasting a lot of yarn, or 2) Carry on. I decided to carry on and finish the towels. Ultimately, I liked the towels with the striped pile better than solid plush pile and decided they'd be featured in the book. The striping makes the towels more interesting. Both 8 epi and 16 epi options are given in the project instructions.

Tensioning

As I mentioned earlier, even if you have a second warp beam on your loom, I recommend using a weighted tensioning system for supplemental warp pile weaves. So if you've been using a second beam up to now, go back and review the warping system described in Chapter 2. My tensioning system is simple to make: just two 3-foot long pieces of aluminum electrical conduit pipe propped up at each end on pieces of wood and secured in place with bungee cords. The warps can be spread across the pipes and will feed smoothly over them as the weaving progresses. Once the back apron rod (holding the the ground warp) reaches the back beam, I remove the tensioning system and let the weighted supplemental warps hang over the back apron rod.

I strongly recommend using the aluminum conduit pipe because it is very smooth and inexpensive. You could use large-diameter wooden dowels, but I've found that any rough spots on the dowels will catch random warp threads. Don't use PVC pipe: It flexes easily at these smaller diameters, which can affect your supplemental warp tension. **(See Photo 1.)**

Weaving the Cloth

As you weave, you will alternate weaving loop picks on the top and bottom of the cloth, with 2 picks of plain weave between each loop pick. To make each loop pick, you will treadle a supplemental warp pick, insert a dowel in the space between the lifted supplemental warp ends (top loop) and the plain weave warp or between the plain-weave warp ends and the lowered supplemental warp ends (bottom loop), weaving 2 plain-weave picks between each loop pick, beating hard to lock in the pile loops.

I recommend using wooden dowels to create your pile loops. I initially bought $^3/_{16}$" diameter steel rod at the hardware store, thinking it would make terrific inserts for pile picks. While the steel rods were strong and pulled out of the loops very easily, I was disappointed to find that the rod's weight and slippery surface prevented me from beating in the loop picks tightly enough. The rods kept popping away from the fell line and, on my countermarch loom, would try to roll toward the beater. Wooden dowels stay in place much better.

I wove the project towels with dowels of two different diameters: $^3/_{16}$" and $^1/_8$". In the project picture, the pile for the folded towel on the left is woven with the $^3/_{16}$" dowels, resulting in large fluffy loops. The $^1/_8$" dowels make

To calculate the total amount of yarn needed for all of the supplemental warps:

(375" warp length × 128 ends) divided by 36" = 1,333 yards for the supplemental warps

There are two colors of yarn, used in equal proportions in the supplemental warps, so

1,333 yd/2 = 667 yards (rounded up) of each supplemental warp color

Remember to wind your supplemental warps in 2" sections. The stripes in these towels are 4" wide, so each stripe section requires 2 supplemental warp chains in the same color. Remember that there is 1 supplemental warp for every 2 background plain-weave warps, so each 2" supplemental warp chain will contain 16 ends.

A Confession

Having told you several times now that terry-cloth has one pile warp between every 2 ground warps, I need to confess. When I started weaving these towels, the pile sections were separating into narrow horizontal stripes. No matter how hard I beat, the stripes were still there. I beat harder, tried different dowel configurations, and kept saying "*Why is this striping?!!*" Finally the light bulb went on. I had wound the supplemental warp ends at 16 epi instead of 8 epi and threaded them between every ground warp end instead of between every 2 ground warp ends. Good grief! The combined warp was simply tidy little loops in the other towel. Cut the pile dowels about 4" longer than the width of your piece so about 2" of dowel sticks out on each side of the warp. Sand them with fine sandpaper to remove any rough spots that can catch on the warp, and sand the cut ends smooth. Some articles recommend lightly waxing the dowels as well, but I haven't found waxing makes a big enough difference to be worth the effort.

You need a set of at least 6 dowels so that you can always leave 4 dowels in place as you pull the ones closest to you (farthest from the fell) to make the next set of loops. The longer you can leave the dowels in place, the more plain weave picks there are to stabilize the loops when the dowels are removed.

IMPORTANT NOTE: Never, never, never remove all the dowels before advancing your warps. Removing all of the dowels will cause the most recently woven loops to pull out because of the weight on the pile warp! Also, do not yank or pull on the supplemental warps without the dowels in place. If you accidently pull out a set of loops (and believe me, you will only do this once), remove the weights from the supplemental warps, then unweave the ground cloth picks, letting the pile loops pull out, until you get to the plain-weave picks after the last section of intact loops. Carefully weave 2 loop sequences (top and bottom loops plus 2 plain-weave picks between each) then replace the weights on the supplemental warps, and carry on. The tensioning system will provide enough tension to weave these few picks. If you try to re-weight the warps before anchoring the supplemental warps with dowels, you run the risk of pulling out even more pile picks.

The Weaving Sequence

Start all terry-cloth by weaving a plain-weave section to lock in the supplemental warp before you start weaving the pile, regardless of whether you want plain-weave hems on your project. Note on the project draft that Treadles 3, 4, 5 and 6 all weave pile and complete a full cycle of 2 pile picks on top with 2 pile picks on bottom. Treadles 3 and 5 make loops on top of the cloth, and treadles 4 and 6 make loops on the bottom. The weaving sequence goes like this:

- To weave the first pile pick, open the supplemental warp shed on treadle 3 and place your dowel between the raised supplemental warps and the ground cloth warps, release the treadle, and pull the beater forward, squeezing the dowel firmly against the fell line. Leave the beater against the dowel and press the treadle for the first ground-cloth pick. Keeping your foot on the treadle, release the beater, throw the shuttle for the first ground cloth pick, close the shed, and beat firmly followed by a second quick, hard beat. This snugs the first ground-cloth pick up against the dowel. Change sheds for the second ground-cloth pick, throw the shuttle, re-

lease the treadle, and beat firmly.

- Open the supplemental warp shed on treadle 4 (lowers the supplemental warps to back side of the ground cloth), place another dowel between the supplemental warps and ground cloth warps, press the dowel into place, and then weave the 2 plain-weave picks as you did after the previous pile pick.

- Weave the loop picks on treadles 5 (top loops) and 6 (bottom loops), following each with 2 plain-weave picks as described above.

- Once you have all your dowels holding loops, start removing the 2 dowels closest to you (farthest from the fell line), one from the top loops and one from the bottom loops, in preparation for weaving the next set of loops. If you have 6 dowels, you will be leaving the 4 most recently placed dowels in place. Once you remove the 2 dowels, give a couple more firm, sharp beats to close any gaps.

- Continue weaving the sequence of pile and plain-weave picks, alternating loop rows on the top and bottom of the cloth. (If you make a mistake and weave 2 loop picks in a row on either side of the cloth, you will see have a loop-free gap in the ground cloth.) Keep rotating dowels forward from the loop rows closest to you.

IMPORTANT! When weaving the plain-weave picks, make sure your weft thread doesn't wrap around the dowels! If it does, you will have loops of weft along your selvedge edges. **(See Photo 2.)**

Photo 2. Dowels in place in pile loops

Some Weaving Tips

- I am right handed, so I pull the dowels out with my right hand. I usually place the dowels in the pile shed so that the left end extends just beyond the selvedge and the dowel on the right extends far enough from the selvedge that I can easily grab the end of the dowel to pull it from the loops. It will take a bit of pulling to get the dowel started, and turning the dowel a little as you pull helps move things along. Pull the dowels as straight out to the side from the loops as you can. Lifting up or pulling down as you remove the dowels can pull out the pile loops on the opposite side.

- Your ground warp should be under medium tension, not piano-wire tight. Lighter ground warp tension makes it easier to beat the plain-weave picks and pile picks tightly together. When I advance the ground warp, I find that winding the warp to the front beam until taut and then backing off one click of the pawl on my fabric beam works well. You will need to experiment with your loom.

- Your supplemental warps should have just enough weight to keep them from flopping around loosely and from catching on the ground warps as they move from the top layer to bottom layer and back. Start with less weight and add more in small increments if you need it.

- If your pile loops become substantially shorter when you pull out the dowels, either you have too much weight on your supplemental warps or you've removed too many dowels. If you're using at least 6 dowels and leaving 4 in place at all times, you need to decrease the weight on your supplemental warp.

- Because you've sett your fabric to make room for the pile, your plain-weave selvedges are going to look like the weave is too open. However, once you wet-finish the terry-cloth and toss it in the dryer to tumble dry, they will close up nicely. The selvedges also wear better if turned and stitched, so I recommend weaving with a 1" selvedge that can be turned and machine stitched before you hem the ends.

STEP BY STEP INSTRUCTIONS

Step 1 Wind 288 warp threads 3 yd long of the background warp. Wind 8 separate supplemental warp bouts of 16 threads each, 7 yd long. Wind 4 of these bouts in teal and 4 in yellow. Set the supplemental warp bouts aside. Thread the background warps according to the directions in Chapter 2, following the draft in Figure 1.

Step 2 Lay supplemental warps on the loom as described in Chapter 2. Thread the supplemental warps on shafts 1 and 2 following the draft. Space the supplemental warps across the background warp as follows: Start the first

Project at a Glance: Terry-cloth Towels

STRUCTURE
Terry-cloth.

EQUIPMENT
4-shaft loom, 18" weaving width; 8-dent reed; 1 shuttle with bobbin; 6 wooden dowels ⅛" or ³⁄₁₆" diameter and 22"–24" long.

YARNS
Background warp: 10/2 pearl cotton (4,200 yd/lb), teal, 864 yd.
Supplemental warp: 8/2 cottolin, teal and yellow, 512 yd each.
Weft: 10/2 pearl cotton, teal, 512 yd.

(I used WEBS Valley Cotton Line: 10/2 pearl cotton, # 2746 Dark Teal; 8/2 cottolin, #2746 Dark Teal and #1405 Autumn Blonde.)

WARP LENGTH
Background warp: 288 ends 3 yd (allows 7" for take-up, 32" for sampling and loom waste).
Supplemental warp: 128 ends (8 sections of 16 ends each) 8 yd long.

SETTS
Warp: 16 epi (2/dent in an 8-dent reed) for background cloth. In pile sections, sley 2 background warps plus 1 supplemental warp end per dent.
Weft: 16 ppi (ground cloth and pile picks combined).

DIMENSIONS
Width in the reed: 18".
Woven length (measured under tension on the loom): 58".
Finished size after washing: 2 towels about 15" x 25".

supplemental warp 16 background warp ends from the edge. Bundle those first background warp threads and push to the side. Thread the supplemental warp chains according to Figure 1, with 1 supplemental warp end between every 2 background warp ends. There should be a total of 32 background warps and 16 supplemental warps in each color section. When you finish, there should be 16 background warp threads left to the selvedge.

Step 3 Sley the reed, centering for an 18" weaving width. There will be 2 ends/dent in the background-only areas. The supplemental warp sections will have 2 background warp ends and 1 supplemental warp end per dent.

Step 4 Tie on using your preferred method, including the pattern warps with the background warp in the tie-on groups. Weight the supplemental warp bouts over the back beam. Adjust your background warp tension to match that provided by the weights. (Add weight if you like to weave with more tension).

Step 5 Wind a bobbin of weft yarn. Weave at least 2" with waste yarn to spread the warps, then weave 2" of plain weave for hem. Weave plush for 25" as described in this chapter, treadling according to Figure 6. Weave 2" of plain weave for hem, insert two picks of a contrasting yarn to separate the towels, then weave second towel as you did the first.

Step 6 Cut towels off loom. Machine zig-zag across the fell lines. Handwash in warm water. Machine dry with another towel in dryer.

Step 7 Cut towels apart. Fold the selvedge edges in half and machine stitch along the length. Fold the ends under ½" and then again so the folded edge meets the plush. Machine stitch hems.

Figure 1. Draft

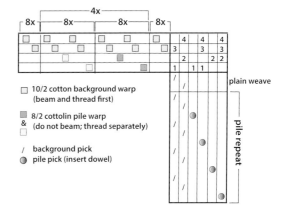

☐ 10/2 cotton background warp
(beam and thread first)

▦ 8/2 cottolin pile warp
& (do not beam; thread separately)
☐

/ background pick
◉ pile pick (insert dowel)

Velvet

VELVET, THE FABRIC OF NOBILITY. While there are conflicting stories of where woven velvet originated, there is archeological evidence of velvet fabric in Egypt dating back to 2000 B.C.E. and of Egyptians exporting velvet to what would become Europe. The Kashmir region of northern India is credited with introducing velvet to the Middle East. During the Renaissance period, the Italian cities of Florence, Venice, and Genoa were renowned for producing beautiful velvet fabrics, and velvet is still considered a luxury fabric today.

Velvet is a supplemental warp pile weave. In the textile industry, velvet pile must be no longer than .36 cm. Fabric with longer pile is called "plush." Silk was historically used as the pile warp for woven velvet because of its sheen and drape, but velvet can be woven from any fiber. The ground cloth can be based on a plain, twill, or satin weave. (Velvet and velveteen are often confused. Both are dense cut pile weave fabrics, but whereas velvet is a supplemental warp fabric, velveteen is a supplemental weft fabric.)

Mechanized looms weave velvet in two layers of plain weave cloth with the supplemental warp threads interlacing back and forth between the two layers. A wire is then passed between the two layers, cutting the supplemental warps, resulting in two lengths of velvet cloth. Handweavers weave velvet in one layer. There are many different types of velvet defined by either the weaving or finishing technique. Handweavers can produce all the types listed here.

Ciselé velvet: Select sections of the pile are cut and other sections of pile are left as loops to create patterns. This is the technique used for the sample in this book.

Voided Velvet: Pattern is produced while weaving by bringing the supplemental pile up in sections to create designs. The ground fabric shows between the areas of pile designs. This is complicated to produce because each supplemental warp thread must be weighted individually to allow for the varying take-up of the supplemental warp as the patterns are woven.

Pile-on-pile: The pile is cut in different lengths to create patterns. As with voided velvet, supplemental warps must be individually weighted to allow for the take-up differences in pile heights.

Nacré velvet: The pile is woven in one or more colors and the ground cloth woven in another color. This creates an iridescent effect on the cloth.

Devoré or burnout velvet: A chemical solution is painted on the pile after weaving to create pattern by dissolving areas of the pile. This technique works best with very short pile and a sheer ground cloth woven of fiber that is not affected by the burnout solution.

Crushed velvet: The finished cloth is wetted, then twisted tightly to create areas where the pile is crushed and creates pattern. This can also be accomplished by firmly pressing the pile in different directions

Embossed velvet: A hot metal stamp or roller with a design is pressed into the pile of the velvet.

Weaving Velvet

The technique for weaving velvet is similar to weaving terry-cloth. The supplemental warps are raised and a dowel inserted in the shed to pull the supplemental warps up into loops. The key difference with velvet is that the supplemental warps are placed between three ground warps, and the ground warps on each side of the supplemental warp are on the same shaft.

In addition, there are three picks of ground cloth between pile picks, starting and ending on the same shaft This creates a small opening for the supplemental warp pile picks, so that when the cloth is removed from the loom, the ground cloth threads squeeze together around the pile.

The first time I wove velvet, I swore I would never do it again. As I cut the pile, some of the cut pieces started to fall out the back of the fabric! I beat harder, which helped a little. I stopped cutting the pile, which helped a lot. I muddled through the sample and blamed the very slippery rayon yarn I was using for the pile shedding problem. Later I learned that, similar to piqué, here are two ways to weave velvet – fast-back and non fast-back.

Fast-back velvet is much more stable. The supplemental warp ends are woven into the ground cloth picks between pile picks. The draft I used in that first piece was for non fast-back velvet, which has the supplemental warp ends floating below the ground cloth. The supplemental warps do not weave into the ground cloth except where they are pulled up for a pile pick. This technique is often used in voided velvet designs where the weaver does not want to see the supplemental warps woven into the ground cloth between sections of pile pattern. A closely sett ground cloth and the weft picks on each side of the pile sandwich the pile pick, holding the pile picks in place. Care must be taken in creating a voided velvet design to make sure the floats on the back between pattern sections do not become too long!

Selecting the Yarns

Silk is the traditional choice for velvet pile warp, but you can use almost any fiber. However, part of the beauty of velvet is the light reflecting off the fibers, so a shiny fiber makes richer-looking velvet. You also want a yarn that when cut, opens nicely into pile. Fine yarns can be used for pile, but you may need to use them doubled, tripled, or more to achieve a lush pile. Think of the multiples of supplemental warp threads working as one warp end.

When treating multiple supplemental warp threads as one pile warp end, the threads can be threaded together in one heddle and sleyed as a unit in the reed. You could thread each individual pile warp thread in its own heddle on the same shaft, but you still need to sley the threads for that pile warp end together in the same dent in the reed. If you are using multiple heddles for a bundle of supplemental warp ends, limit the number of heddles. The heddles will naturally sit next to each other on the shaft, and there can be a point where you create tensioning problems because the warp threads on the outer heddles of the bundle have to travel further than the warp threads at the center of the bundle. Also, your plain-weave threads in the adjacent heddles can be pushed out of alignment so that they no longer travel a straight line from the back of the loom to the reed, causing stretching of those warp ends and problems much like the stretching of selvedge theads if there is too much draw-in. The supplemental warp for the velvet wall hanging project has two lengths of bamboo yarn in each heddle and both are sleyed as if one thread. Sampling is the only way to determine if you need to have multiple lengths of supplemental warp yarn to achieve the desired pile density.

The ground warp yarn should be finer than the supplemental warps, and the ground cloth sett should be calculated as you normally would for whatever weave structure you've selected for the ground fabric: plain weave, twill or satin. See the Appendix for warp sett and length calculation formulas.

Threading and Tie-up

Figure 1 shows the basic fast-back velvet draft. Note that there are always three ground-cloth warps threaded on shafts 3 and 4 between supplemental warps threaded alternately on shafts 1 and 2. This draft shows only one supplemental warp thread per heddle, but you can easily thread two or three supplemental warps per heddle as a unit. If your heddle becomes too crowded with supplemental warp threads, thread the next heddle on the same shaft with the extra supplemental warps for that pile warp unit. (Remember that you still sley all of the supplemental warp threads in that unit together in the same dent on your reed, and the reed should have dents large enough that the supplemental warp threads can move without binding.)

The wide weft picks on the draft are the pile picks where a dowel is inserted to create the pile loops.

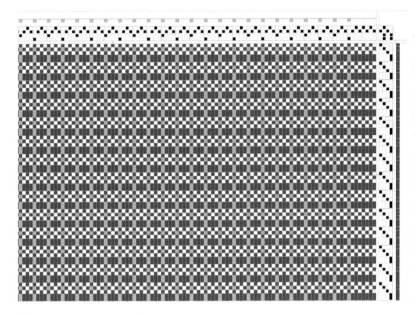

Figure 1. Basic velvet draft

All of the supplemental warp pile picks happen on the top of the fabric. Three picks of the ground fabric are woven between each pile pick. You'll notice on the draft that treadles 1 and 3 are tied up the same. You don't need to do this, but it's easier to keep track of your treadling: treadles 1, 2 & 3 weave the ground picks and treadle 4 weaves the pile pick.

Weighting the Supplemental Warps

For velvet, it's necessary to use small bundles of supplemental warps, each weighted individually. If you use the same color across the width of the fabric, make sure your supplemental warps are in bundles that weave no more than 2" wide. If you have narrow sections of color, the supplemental warp sections can be wound and weighted by color. As you weave, the take-up on the supplemental warps will differ between cut pile and loop pile picks. For the wall hanging project in this chapter, the purple and rust sections have more sections of looped pile and the take-up on these sections is dramatically more than the dark blue sections.

Calculate the supplemental warp lengths the same way as terry-cloth supplemental warp lengths. (Refer to Project 6 and the Appendix.) Add 12" to the calculated supplemental warp length to allow extra warp if you plan to create designs at the loom.

You want to add enough weight so the supplemental warps advance easily and don't catch on the ground cloth warps when weaving plain-weave picks, but not so much weight that the loops want to pull out. For the velvet project, I started with 6 oz of weight per supplemental warp chain. The supplemental warps flopped around and got caught on the ground warps, creating uneven take-up for the pile picks. Increasing the weights to 8 oz per chain solved the problem.

Weaving Steps

Weaving velvet is similar to weaving terry-cloth. (Refer to Chapter 10.) Begin by weaving at least ½" of your chosen ground cloth before beginning the pile weaving; this helps to to lock the supplemental warps in with the ground cloth. For the pile picks, treadle one of the supplemental warps picks, insert the dowel, and press the beater firmly against the dowel. Leave the beater in place against the dowel and change sheds to the first ground cloth shed (always treadle 1). Release the beater and throw your shuttle for the first ground pick. Beat very firmly. Weave the next two ground cloth picks, beating firmly for each pick.

Make sure your weft yarn does not wrap around the dowels at the selvedges. If it does, you will have a little loop of weft at the selvedge. Once you cut the pile, there is no going back to correct a mistake.

Weave a minimum of four sets of three ground picks and one pile pick (you'll have four dowels in place), and weave the three ground picks for the next pile sequence after the fourth dowel and before cutting the pile on the first (closest to you) dowel. After you cut the pile, another firm beat will help tighten up the ground cloth. Use the dowel you just removed for the next pile pick, secure the newly placed dowel by weaving the three ground picks, and then cut the pile on the dowel that is now closest to you. Once the pile is cut, move this dowel to weave the next pile pick sequence. Continue this pattern for the length of the cloth.

Be sure to leave the dowels in place when you advance the warps or you run the risk of pulling out your supplemental pile warps! End your pieces by weaving at least ½" of ground cloth to secure the last supplemental warp picks.

Velvet weaving is slow, but I find the rhythm almost meditative. Don't rush the process, especially when cutting the pile loops! My first traumatic experience with velvet came when I literally broke into a cold sweat as I placed an Exacto knife tip on the dowel and started cutting the piles. One slip could mean cut warp! The rounded handle of the Exacto knife made it harder to control the blade. The blades needed to be very sharp to cleanly cut the pile warps, which meant changing blades often. It got expensive! I got cranky.

Since that first velvet experience, I have discovered disposable box-cutting knives at the hardware store. The blades for these knives are scored so that when the cutting tip gets dull, you break off that section of blade for a new sharp section. The size and rectangular shape of the knife is much easier to hold, and the ability to extend a very short length of blade offers better control. An added bonus is the knives are really inexpensive!

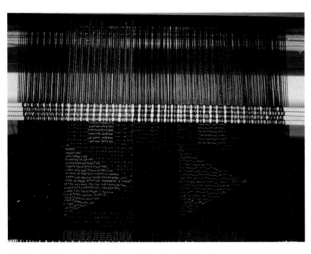

Photo 1. Velvet pile picks with dowels in place

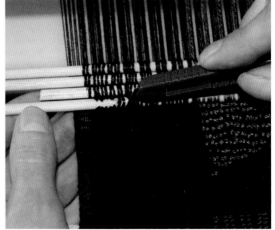

Photo 2. Cutting the pile

If you weave a lot of velvet, you will probably want to invest in cutting tools designed for velvet weaving. Internet research has led me to descriptions and videos showing weavers using special pile-cutting tools, but no sources for purchasing them in the United States. If you really want a velvet-cutting tool, ask a metal machinist to make you fabricate any of the following.

Lengths of metal rod (round or square) with a diameter of ³⁄₁₆" or smaller, and a groove centered along the length of the rod to run your blade along.

Lengths of metal folded in half length-wise into a "v" shape. The open part of the "v" is placed upward in the pile shed and the cutting blade run in the opening. (Handwoven January/February 2010, article by Robin Spady on weaving velvet.)

I saw one tool in a video that I really want but haven't found for purchase. It appears be a rotary cutter or very sharp blade that is in a holder with an extended edge on one side. Holding the extended edge against the rod in the pile shed and running it along the length of the rod cuts all the pile warps quickly. Maybe if I go to Italy someday . . .

Alternating Colors in the Velvet Pile

By alternating the color order of supplemental warps on shafts 1 and 2, you can change colors along the fabric, as shown in Figure 2. Only one color shows on the surface at a time so blocks of colors are possible. The color that is not being used floats on the underside of the ground cloth for the pile pick. By adding another treadle tied up to both supplemental warp shafts (in this case shaft 1 and 2) both colors will show in the pile sections. Note that in this draft, treadles 1 and 2 are tied up for the ground cloth, and are alternated for the ground cloth picks.

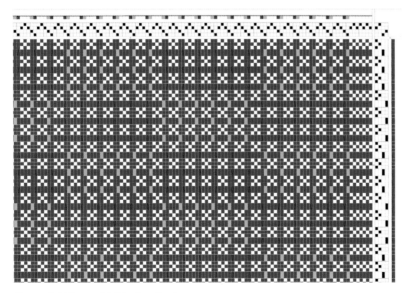

Figure 2. Velvet with blocks of color

Project at a Glance: Velvet Hanging

STRUCTURE
Ciselé velvet.

EQUIPMENT
4-shaft loom, 14" weaving width; 10-dent reed; 1 shuttle with bobbin; 4 wooden dowels 3/16" diameter and 20" long.

YARNS
Background warp: 10/2 pearl cotton (4,200 yd/lb), black, 404 yd.
Supplemental warp: 5/2 bamboo (2,100 yd/lb), blue-black, 336 yd; purple and rust, 168 yd each.
Weft: 10/2 pearl cotton, black, 132 yd.

(I used WEBS Valley Cotton: 10/2 pearl cotton, #8990 Black, and WEBS 5/2 Bamboo, Midnight, Eggplant, and Sienna.)

OTHER MATERIALS
Sewing thread for hems; beads (optional); 15" length of ¼" dowel, painted black, for hanger.

WARP LENGTH
Background warp: 269 ends 1½ yd (allows 3" for take-up, 35" for sampling and loom waste; loom waste includes fringe). **Supplemental warp:** 84 ends (supplemental warp is used doubled; wind 3 warp chains of Midnight, 28 threads each; 1 warp chain each of Sierra and Eggplant, 42 threads each) 4 yd long.

SETTS
Warp: 20 epi (2/dent in a 10-dent reed) for background cloth. In pile sections, sley 2 background warps plus 1 supplemental warp end (2 supplemental warp threads) per dent.
Weft: 20 ppi (ground cloth and pile picks combined).

DIMENSIONS
Width in the reed: 13½".
Woven length (measured under tension on the loom): 16".
Finished size after washing: 1 hanging about 15" x 12" plus 4" fringe at one end.

Figure 3. Draft

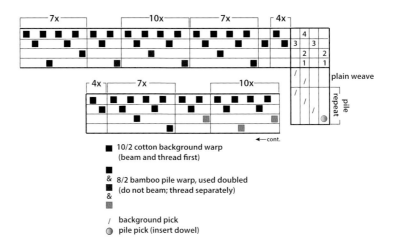

- ■ 10/2 cotton background warp
  (beam and thread first)

- ■
  & 8/2 bamboo pile warp, used doubled
  ■ (do not beam; thread separately)
  &

- ▨
  / background pick
  ◐ pile pick (insert dowel)

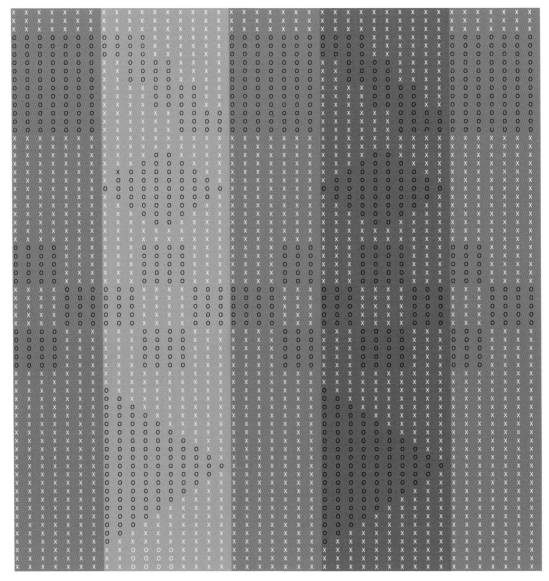

Figure 4. Velvet cutting template

STEP BY STEP INSTRUCTIONS

Step 1 Wind 267 warp threads 3 yd long of the background warp. Wind 5 separate supplemental warp chains, each 4 yd long. Wind 3 of these chains in blue-black, 28 threads each, and 1 chain each in purple and rust, 42 threads each . Set the supplemental warp bouts aside. Thread the background warps according to the directions in Chapter 2, following the draft in Figure 3.

Step 2 Lay supplemental warps on the loom as described in Chapter 2. Thread the supplemental warps on shafts 1 and 2 following the draft. Space the supplemental warps across the background warp as follows: Start the first supplemental warp 9 background warp ends from the edge. Bundle those first background warp threads and push to the side. Thread the supplemental warp chains according to Figure 1, with 1 supplemental warp end (remember that each supplemental warp end is 2 threads) between every 3 background warp ends. There should be a total of 42 background warps and 14 supplemental warp ends in each blue-black section and a total of 63 background warp ends and 21 supplemental warp ends in the other two sections. When you finish, there should be 8 background warp threads left to the selvedge.

Step 3 Sley the reed, centering for a 13½" weaving width. There will be 2 ends/dent in the background-only areas. The supplemental warp sections will have 2 background warp ends and 1 supplemental warp end (2 supplemental warp threads) per dent.

Step 4 Tie on using your preferred method, including the pattern warps with the background warp in the tie-on groups. Weight the supplemental warp bouts over the back beam. Adjust your background warp tension to match that provided by the weights. (Add weight if you like to weave with more tension).

Step 5 Wind a bobbin of weft yarn. Weave at least 4" with waste yarn to spread the warps, then weave 2" of plain weave for to help lock in the first pile picks. Weave a section of pile, cutting all of the loops so pile runs from selvedge to selvedge. Follow the chart, Figure 4, for creating pattern by contrasting cut and uncut pile or make up your own designs. End by weaving 3 inches of plain weave for casing for hanger.

Step 6 Cut hanging off loom. Machine stitch across the fell lines on both ends. On the fringe end, knot fringe tightly against the file line in bundles of 4 ends. Wet-finish and dry as described in insert.

Step 7 Trim the excess warp ends close to the fell line on the casing end. To make the casing: Turn the raw edge ½" to the wrong side and press. Turn again so the pressed edge meets the edge of the pile. Handstitch the pressed edge.

Step 8 To make the hanger cord, cut eight 36" long lengths of bamboo yarn in blue-black. Tie an overhand knot in one end and divide into two bundles of four lengths each. Attach to a post or doorknob and twist each length until they start to ply back on each other. Tie an overhand knot in the end and let go. The two lengths will ply together. Measure your length needed, tie to the hanger and then cut the excess twisted cord.

Step 9 Decorate with beads or objects of your choice.

Wet-finishing Velvet

Wet-finishing velvet helps to move the warp and weft closer together and the cut pile yarns to bloom, but it is very traumatic to wash your velvet. Wet velvet looks like a wet cat. It must be carefully laid flat to dry, pile side up, and gently stroked to coax the pile into standing order.

However, if you just can't bear to wet the velvet in a tub of water, I've found that spritzing the back side of the fabric with water until the it is very damp and then laying the piece flat to dry with the pile side up works very well. You can even spritz the pile side to encourage the cut pile yarn to bloom more.

Velvet Weaving in Venice

It all started in 2017, when my music-loving husband, Marty, discovered **Within Temptation,** a symphonic rock band from the Netherlands. We streamed a concert off the internet and I innocently said I'd go to Europe to see the band perform. Marty excitedly told me that the band had a European concert tour planned for 2018! Well, we were overdue for a vacation, and the planning began.

We reviewed our respective work schedules and the band's tour dates, selecting the show in Milan, Italy, in December 2018. With date and location selected, I searched the internet for weaving studios in northern Italy. Suddenly, my Facebook newsfeed showed a post by Tessitura Bevilacqua in Venice (sometimes those Facebook algorithms are handy). A quick trip to Bevilacqua's website sealed the deal. I proposed an article to *Handwoven* magazine about velvet weaving in Venice, convinced Marty to take photos, and arranged for a tour of the studio.

Our hotel in Venice was located by the Santa Maria del Giglio church. We checked in and headed out to explore. Imagine my surprise as I looked across the piazza and saw the retail shop for Bevilacqua! **(See photo 1.)** It

Photo 1: *Bevilacqua* retail store near Santa Maria del Giglio church, Venice, Italy

was destiny! I left Marty taking photographs of the church and popped into the shop. It was packed with luscious velvets. I asked (using my very limited Italian and a lot of gestures) the woman at the counter if she could mark where the studio was on my map of Venice. She kindly circled the location, and I felt confident about finding the studio the next day.

All transportation within Venice is by boat (water bus, water taxi, gondola) or on foot. The public entrance to Tessitura Bevilacqua is on the Grand Canal and requires taking a water taxi. We were instructed to go to the employee entrance in the back of the building for the tour. Armed with my map, we took the water bus to the stop nearest the studio and headed out on the short walk to the studio entrance, which, according to the instructions, was "behind the church." "Streets" in Venice are narrow sidewalks and canals between close-set buildings, so seeing landmarks can be tricky. We found the church and circled it, but no studio. We studied the map, backtracked, and finally found the unassuming back entrance marked with a tiny sign. **(See photos 2 and 3.)** I rang the bell, waited, rang again, and waited, and a young woman opened the door. I think she asked us what we wanted, but as I mentioned earlier, I speak very little Italian. In English, I said we were there for a tour with Maddalena. "Maddalena? Un momento!" she said and shut the door, which, frankly, was not reassuring at the time. A couple minutes later the door reopened and a young woman speaking fluent English welcomed us. Whew! We really were in the right spot.

Photo 2: *Bevilacqua* workshop building and back entrance

Photo 3: The small, unassuming sign indicating we were in the right place!

Tessitura is Italian for "weaving." Tessitura Bevilacqua (pronounced "Bee-LOCK-wa") was established in 1875 by Luigi Bevilacqua. Luigi purposefully purchased the building because it once housed the Silk Weaving School of the Republic of Venice, and all the original looms and equipment were included with the building. The Silk Weaving School was established in 1488 and was part of the Silk Weavers Guild of Venice. Guilds in Venice at that time were not like our Weaving Guilds today. The Venetian Guilds were organizations that regulated manufacture, quality control, worker training, working conditions, and wages/pensions for various industries—much like modern labor unions. Guilds were established during the Renaissance (1400–1600) for every industry, from painters of art to furniture makers to weaving cloth and tailoring. The Guilds flourished until 1805, when the Venetian Guild system was abolished by Napoleonic decree and the Silk Weaving School closed. When the Silk Weaving School was in operation, all three floors of the building housed looms and weavers. In 2018, the main floor contained 18 of the original looms plus other original weaving equipment still in use. Tessitura Bevilacqua employed eight weavers and two apprentices.

We followed Maddalena down a short hallway and entered the workshop—it was like walking into a time capsule. Shelves stacked with gray paper lined the walls from floor to ceiling. These stacks are part of the archive of weaving pattern dobby punch cards that are now used as reference for the patterned velvets Bevilacqua is most famous for. **(See photo 4.)** Incongruously, mounted on the shelves was a small flat-screen television, and we watched a short video on the steps of preparing the warps and weaving velvet. The two huge warping reels (vertical and horizontal) in the photo date back to the Silk Weaving School and are still in use. According to Maddalena, it's believed that the warping reel was invented by Leonardo da Vinci (1452–1519).

Photo 4: A portion of the archive of 3,500 sets of dobby punch cards that contain patterned velvet designs. Each tag marks one set of pattern punch cards.

Photo 5: Sample of punch cards draped over an old Jacquard dobby head. Each hole in the card weaves a tuft of pile. Each row of holes weaves a pick of pile. Each card weaves 1 mm of fabric.

Photo 6: Tools used to create the punch cards. Pins are inserted in the template according to a graphed image. The template is inserted into a card press with a blank card. Then the card press applies pressure so the pins cut through the card.

Photo 7: Jacquard dobby head and pattern cards installed above a loom

After Luigi purchased the building, he had Jacquard dobby heads installed on many of the looms. Invented in 1804 by Joseph Jacquard, the dobby head mechanized the use of punch cards **(see photos 5 and 6)** to create the pile patterns in the voided/patterned velvet fabrics. The use of punch cards for weaving patterns was originally devised by Jacques d'Vauconson in 1745, and the cards/warp threads were manipulated by hand. The Jacquard dobby head **(see photo 7)** automatically advances the cards and allows individual warp threads to be raised with a single treadle pressed by the weaver.

Bevilacqua's specialty is "soprarizzo" (curly) velvet—voided velvet where pile is pulled up into patterns with both cut and looped pile and the base cloth shows between the areas with pile. **(See photo 8.)** The designs are highly detailed and complex. When the supplemental warp is raised for a pile pick, the weaver inserts a rod between the base cloth and supplemental warps to create loops on the surface. After several rods are placed, the weaver cuts the pile in specific locations across the warp according

Photo 8: Soprarizzo velvet. Note the detail in the design. Darker pattern areas are cut pile, and lighter pattern areas are looped pile. Areas of cut vs. looped pile are cut by hand according to the pattern..

Photo 10: A loom dressed for patterned velvet. Supplemental warps are the threads coming up from the bobbin rack below the loom and placed between the base cloth threads (gold threads on loom).

to the pattern. Then the rod is pulled out, and a row of cut vs. looped pile is left on the fabric. When the same hue of yarn is used in a design, the cut pile appears darker in color, and the looped pile looks lighter because the loops reflect light.

The looms are set up by velvet type and pattern. Due to the patterning, soprarizzo velvet requires a system where each individual supplemental warp thread can be manipulated and allows for different take-up of each pile thread. This is accomplished by winding the supplemental warps on individual bobbins that are held in a rack below the base cloth warp. **(See photo 9.)** Each bobbin holds two threads of fine 20/22 silk thread spun specifically for Bevilacqua at a mill in Italy. The numbers 20/22 represent the number of very fine singles yarns (20) that are plied together into the final size of the yarn (22). When cut, the large number of plies blooms into a dense velvet pile. Each bobbin is individually weighted to control the spin of the bobbin as the yarn advances. The bobbin racks hold up to 800 bobbins for a total of 1,600 pile warps, depending on the design. **(See photo 10.)** Due to the width of the looms, the velvet fabric is no wider than 67 cm (about 26 inches),

Photo 9: Supplemental warp bobbins in the bobbin rack. Each bobbin holds two supplemental warp threads. Note the small lead weight on each bobbin as a counterweight.

Photo 11: Each supplemental warp thread is threaded through one long cord/heddle that leads up to the Jacquard head, so individual threads can be raised independently to create pile pattern in the fabric. The base cloth warps are threaded in the shafts, which are tied up to the dobby head.

which is about an arm's length. Each set of bobbin threads is threaded individually in long heddle cords that are connected to the Jacquard head above the loom. **(See photo 11.)** The base cloth warp contains 3,000–6,000 threads, depending on sett/size of the yarn used, and the base cloth warps are threaded through heddles on the shafts. The shafts are also connected to the Jacquard head.

The base cloth yarn is typically a fine linen thread but can be silk or cotton depending on the commission or use for the fabric. The base cloth warp is wound on the loom's back beam, and the supplemental warps are brought up from the bobbins between the base cloth warp threads. In a typical day, about 20–30 cm (8-12 inches) of soprarizzo velvet can be woven. Each loom is warped with 20 meters (66 feet) of base cloth warp

Photo 12: Selvedge to selvedge velvet loom setup. The red threads wound on the upper warp beam are the supplemental pile warp. The gold base cloth threads are wound onto the lower warp beam.

Photo 13: Weaving selvedge to selvedge velvet. The long pins in the fabric pull the pile warps up into loops.

Photo 14: Cutting the pile on pin closest to the weaver. Cut pile length is 1 mm. After a row is cut, the pin is removed and used to weave the next row of pile.

length and 30 meters (98 feet) of supplemental pile warp length. Prepping the loom for a new design typically involves two or three weavers and can take six months of work, from creating the pattern on graph paper, to cutting the punch cards, to winding the warps and dressing the loom before the actual weaving can begin.

When we toured in 2018, two weavers were working on a commission for 740 meters of selvedge to selvedge velvet to be used in the restoration of the Dresden Palace in Germany. I encourage you to do an internet search on the Dresden Palace restoration, completed in 2021, and view the fabulous velvets in situ as curtains, wall coverings, and upholstery. Breathtaking!

Because the supplemental warp for selvedge to selvedge velvet pile has equal thread take-up across the width of the fabric, it's not necessary to individually wind the supplemental warp threads onto bobbins. Instead, selvedge to selvedge velvet uses two warp beams—the lower beam for the base cloth warp and the upper beam for the pile. **(See photo 12.)** Additionally, these looms do not use a dobby head—four conventional shafts (two for pile and two for base cloth) are all that are needed.

Photo 15: The public showroom accessible from the Grand Canal

For each pile pick, the pile warp is raised and a rod is inserted between the supplemental warp and the base cloth warp. Then three picks of the base cloth are woven (using a fly shuttle) with a very firm beat to lock the pile into place. After six to eight pile rods are placed, the weaver cuts the row of pile loops on the rod closest to her. The cut pile length on this velvet is 1 mm (yes, 1 millimeter). The average woven length per day of plain velvet is half a meter. **(See photos 13 & 14.)**

Our wonderful tour ended in the front showroom. **(See photo 15.)** The walls were lined with historical photos and amazing velvet fabrics. The average price of the velvet was €1500–€2000 per meter. Pillows, handbags, and other items were also displayed. If you can't make it to Italy, the weaving studio has a marvelous website (in English or Italian) with many informative stories and videos of velvet weaving in action at www.luigi-bevilacqua.com.

And in case you are wondering—the concert was wonderful too!

Woven Shibori

SHIBORI IS A JAPANESE RESIST-DYE TECHNIQUE in which a piece of cloth is stitched, folded, tied, and/or wrapped before dyeing to create a pattern. In traditional shibori, rows of stitching are drawn tight to create patterns in the cloth where dye cannot penetrate. The area where the dye doesn't penetrate is called the resist. There are many different techniques for traditional shibori, and each has its own name.

kanoko shibori – Familiar to those in the U.S. as our stereotypical tie-dye, thread (we often use rubber bands) is wound tightly around sections of cloth in a circular manner, creating circular designs on the cloth surface

miura shibori – Also known as looped binding, a small section of cloth is gathered and thread is tightly looped twice around the gathered cloth. Then the thread is carried to another gathered section, looped, then carried to the next section. Wrapping continues in this manner until all the desired sections are gathered and tied. The thread is not knotted between sections.

kumo shibori – Cloth is pleated and then bound in small sections with thread.

nui shibori – A running stitch is sewn in the cloth in a pattern. The stitching is drawn tight and tied. This is the technique we emulate with woven shibori.

arashi shibori – Fabric is wrapped diagonally around a pole and then gathered and bound to the pole by tightly wrapping thread around the pole/fabric many times, creating a wave-like pattern.

itajime shibori – Cloth is folded many times then sandwiched between two shapes of wood and then clamped. Different shapes of wood create different designs in the resist area.

Years ago, I took a class in traditional Japanese shibori and decided that while the patterns were fabulous, the stitching process was too tedious for my temperament. However, woven shibori is fast and fun!

Most woven shibori is done with a supplemental weft that interlaces with the warp at intervals across the warp. After weaving and before dyeing, the supplemental wefts are drawn tight from side to side to create the resist areas. (We call them "draw cords.")

Woven shibori with a supplemental warp has the draw cord interlacing lengthwise with the ground cloth. The supplemental warps are drawn tight from end to end to create resist areas of pattern running the length of the cloth. Both supplemental weft and supplemental warp shibori can be used alone or together in cloth design. But this is a book about supplemental warps, so we will explore supplemental warp shibori.

Be forewarned: Woven shibori is an adventure in seeing what happens, especially when you first try it. As weavers, we are used to precision—a weave structure is repeatable and predictable. Woven shibori is free-form exploration. It's about reveling in the unexpected. Different gathering techniques, different dyes, and different weights of background cloth yarns can all yield different results. Dye may migrate differently than expected. Pieces can be similar, but will have individual personalities. So be prepared to celebrate the unpredictable and have some fun!

Woven shibori is a good place to start with supplemental warps. You need far fewer supplemental warp threads than other supplemental warp weave structures. It also gives you the opportunity to easily observe what is happening with the supplemental warp and familiarize yourself with warping and weaving supplemental warps.

A Woven Shibori Draft

Let's look at the draft for the woven shibori project, Figure 1.

This project utilizes two supplemental warp chains of only 8 ends each. The base cloth is plain weave on shafts 3 and 4 with the draw cords on shafts 1 and 2. The draw cords alternate floating on the top and bottom of the fabric and look like a long sewn running stitch.

Your draw cords should be smooth, strong threads. I like using white 8/2 Tencel **(see Photo 1)**. It's very strong and has the added bonus of being slightly slippery so the draw cords pull smoothly when pleating. I strongly suggest using white yarn for the draw cords. Some colored yarns can bleed dye when wet and then that dye can absorb into your piece. Yes, I found this out the hard way. Monofilament fishing line also works (about a 6–8 pound test), but it's trickier to work with, harder to see, and it's difficult to tie the knots that keep the pleating cords tight during dyeing. I don't recommend it.

When the cloth is removed from the loom and the draw cord warps are pulled tight and tied, the fabric gathers and pleats. Dye is absorbed into areas where the fabric is in contact with the dye bath and the pleated areas resist taking up dye.

You can create different patterns by alternating the draw cords on shafts 1 and 2 or having all the draw cords on one shaft. Having the draw cords all on the same shaft will create bars of color/resist. Alternating between shafts creates different patterns. The number of warp threads between draw cords and the number of picks woven all affect the patterns created. Longer floats create more irregular patterns. Shorter floats create more defined patterns.

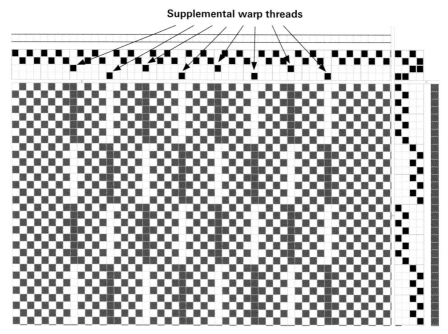

Supplemental warp threads

Figure 1. Woven shibori draft

Photo 1. Shibori scarf on the loom with Tencel drawcords

The fun doesn't end with just the gathering techniques—you can dye the piece with the draw cords pulled tight in one dye bath, then pull out the draw cords and over-dye the entire piece in a second color. The undyed resist areas will become the color of the second dye bath and the dyed areas become a combination of the original dye color and the second dye color. (Use your color wheel to make sure you get a color you like on your over-dyed sections!) Try laying the gathered piece in a shallow pan with dye so only one side absorbs dye. Then flip the piece and lay in a second shallow pan with a different color dye and that side absorbs the second color dye. When you undo the supplemental warp gathering cords, the colors can show on one or both sides, depending on the gathers. Undoing the draw cords is almost like opening a gift—you can guess what is going to happen but opening the piece delivers the real surprise. If you find this technique intriguing, you will love the book *Woven Shibori* by Catharine Ellis, which explores supplemental weft and warp shibori techniques in depth. (See Resources in the back of this book.)

After your piece is dyed, snip away the draw cords, leaving a plain weave cloth with a shibori design.

Tying The Resist Patterns

When you take the cloth off the loom, at each end of the piece, tie together all of the draw cords in each section using overhand knots tied close to the fell line. (If you have a very wide section of draw cords, you may tie them in two or more bundles.) **THIS IS INCREDIBLY IMPORTANT!** *If you fail to knot the draw cords together in bundles* **on both ends before** *gathering, you can accidentally pull your draw cords out of the fabric when*

you start pulling! Make sure that you don't include any of the fringe ends from the underlying fabric in the knots for the supplemental warp draw cords. I also recommend tying the draw cords together before you knot any fringes for the ground cloth so you don't accidently include draw cords in the fringe knots.

Now start pulling on the draw cords, alternating between the draw cord sections and working/pushing the gathers toward the middle of the cloth from each end. Push the gathers together as tightly as you can. The tighter the gathers are pushed together, the cleaner the resist pattern will be.

After gathering the fabric you will have long lengths of draw cords on each end of the fabric. *Working on one end and one section at a time,* cut the excess draw cord yarn about 8 inches from the fell line of the fabric. Cutting the excess length gets it out of the way for dyeing. Leaving the draw cords a little longer than the background cloth fringe makes it easier to find the draw cords for removal after dyeing.

Now separate the draw cords into smaller bundles of four ends each. Push the fabric into gathers as tight as you can without pulling on the draw cords, and tie overhand knots in the draw cords right up against the end of the fabric. Repeat the process on the other end. Tying the cords tightly against the fabric will help keep the resist pattern running right to the edge. Of course, the worst thing that will happen is the ends of the pattern section will absorb more dye, resulting in less resist pattern, which isn't all bad if you are consistent and both ends match.

Take your time when pulling the draw cords and gathering the cloth. Make sure all of the cords in a section are drawn tight and the gathers are really packed together the

Photo 2. Gathered fabric, ready to dye

entire (now much shorter) length of the piece. It's very easy to have gathers that are less compact in the center and on the ends, which will produce less pattern definition in those areas when the cloth is dyed.

Dyeing the Fabric

As with any dye project, use utensils and pots that are reserved for dyeing. Anything used for dyeing should not be used for food. Wear safety equipment such as a dust mask when working with dye power, and use rubber gloves and an apron while dyeing. Cover countertops with plastic or newspaper. Keep in mind that many dyes and mordants contain chemicals that should not be dumped down the drain—especially if you have a septic system. Follow the dye manufacturer's instructions for adding mordants (chemical catalysts that help the dye form a chemical bond with the fabric).

Use a large pot for dyeing. If you are using a fiber that needs heat to absorb the dye, enamel coated canning pots, stock pots, or roasters are great; good sized, light weight, and inexpensive. If you have an uncoated pot, make sure it's stainless steel, as aluminum or cast iron pots can cause a color change when dyeing.

For this project, I used Dye-lishus cotton from New World Textiles. Dye-lishus cotton has been pre-treated so that any kind of dye works on it—natural dyes, acid or direct dyes, Kool-aid, or even food coloring—without having to pre-mordant the fabric or add mordant to the dye bath. The sample pictured was dyed with Jacquard Acid dye, which is normally only for animal fibers but works on Dye-lishus cotton. One caveat that I have discovered:

Acid dyes give a more pastel shade on Dye-lishus cotton. Direct dyes formulated for plant fibers and natural dyes give more saturated color.

Dye-lishus cotton also only needs hot tap water (their instructions recommend 80-120 degrees, but I've found 100-120 degrees initial temperature is best) to absorb the dye. No need to have a pot simmering away on the stove or to steam the fabric. It also means you can use plastic tubs and bins to hold the dye stock.

While you prepare the dye pot, let the gathered fabric soak in warm water for 20 to 30 minutes or more. *The fabric **must** be thoroughly wet before dyeing.* Water needs to be absorbed up into the resist areas in the gathers. It seems counter-intuitive, but the water in the resist areas will help keep the dye from wicking up into the resist areas.

Dissolve the dye powder in 1 cup of hot water and add to the water in the dye pot, pop in the pleated fabric, and let it sit. The longer you let the fabric rest in the dye bath, the more dye will be absorbed and the darker the shade of color.

Regardless of the type of yarn used, don't squish or fold the fabric to fit into a small pot—the dye can migrate into the resist areas.

Important Reminder: *Make sure your draw cords are white yarn!* I found out the hard way that if any color bleeds off the draw cords during the wetting/dyeing process, the Dye-lishus cotton will happily absorb that color and you will have some unexpected design elements.

If your fabric floats on the surface of the dye bath, use an old plate or jars partially filled with water and capped

to weigh it down so that that it floats below the surface of the dye bath. Don't weight it down so much that it rests on the bottom of the pot, as that will create an unplanned resist.

Resist stirring, poking, prodding, squishing, squeezing, or any other rigorous handling of the fabric while it's in the dye pot. Too much movement can cause the dye to migrate to resist areas. Just let the fabric float in the dye until it is the color you want. Remember, the color of the wet fabric will be much, much darker than the color when it's dry. To check the color, squeeze the fringes, not the pleated fabric as that could force dye into the resist areas.

When removing the fabric from the pot, let the excess dye run off into the dye pot. Do not squeeze or wring the pleated fabric. Rinse the pleated fabric under cool running water to remove excess dye until the water runs clear. *Gently* squeeze the fabric to remove some of the water. *Then* remove the draw cords by carefully cutting the knots on one end of the fabric and holding the draw cords on the opposite end, pull on the end of the fabric until it is completely open. Then grasp the draw cord knots on the opposite end of the fabric and pull the draw cords completely out of the fabric. Finish rinsing under running water, then squeeze to remove water. To remove more water, roll the scarf in an old towel and compress the roll. (Stepping on it works.) Unroll and lay the scarf flat to dry on a clean surface.

If you are using any other kind of yarn than Dye-lishus cotton, please be sure to select the correct dye for your yarn and use the required mordant according to the manufacturer's instructions. Acid dyes are for animal fibers including wool, alpaca, silk, llama. Direct dyes are for plant fibers including cotton, linen, hemp, tencel (lyocell), rayon, and bamboo. Natural dyes work on both animal and plant fibers but need different mordants depending on the fiber.

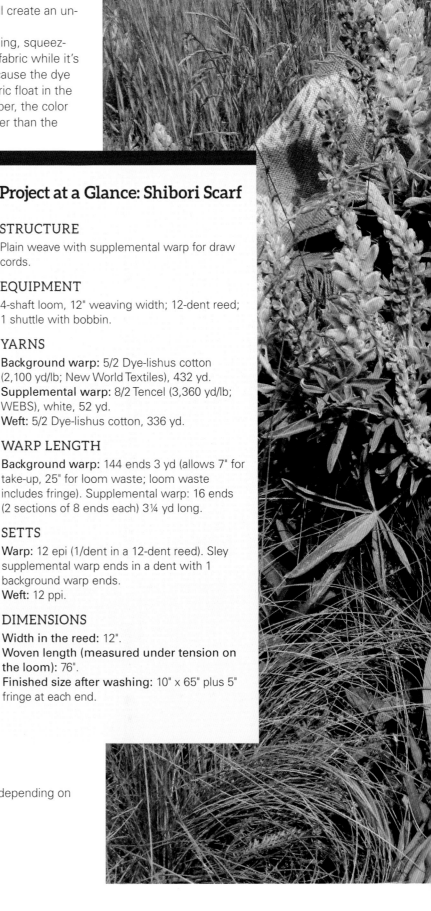

Project at a Glance: Shibori Scarf

STRUCTURE
Plain weave with supplemental warp for draw cords.

EQUIPMENT
4-shaft loom, 12" weaving width; 12-dent reed; 1 shuttle with bobbin.

YARNS
Background warp: 5/2 Dye-lishus cotton (2,100 yd/lb; New World Textiles), 432 yd.
Supplemental warp: 8/2 Tencel (3,360 yd/lb; WEBS), white, 52 yd.
Weft: 5/2 Dye-lishus cotton, 336 yd.

WARP LENGTH
Background warp: 144 ends 3 yd (allows 7" for take-up, 25" for loom waste; loom waste includes fringe). Supplemental warp: 16 ends (2 sections of 8 ends each) 3¼ yd long.

SETTS
Warp: 12 epi (1/dent in a 12-dent reed). Sley supplemental warp ends in a dent with 1 background warp ends.
Weft: 12 ppi.

DIMENSIONS
Width in the reed: 12".
Woven length (measured under tension on the loom): 76".
Finished size after washing: 10" x 65" plus 5" fringe at each end.

STEP BY STEP INSTRUCTIONS

Step 1 Wind 144 warp threads 3 yd long of the background warp. Wind 2 separate supplemental warp bouts of 8 threads each, 3¼ yd long. Set the supplemental warp bouts aside. Thread the background warps according to the directions in Chapter 2, following the draft in Figure 2.

Step 2 Lay supplemental warps on the loom as described in Chapter 2. Thread the supplemental warps on shafts 1 and 2 following the draft. Space the supplemental warps across the background warp as follows:

Start the first supplemental warp 28 background warp ends from the edge. Bundle the background warp threads and push to the side. Thread the first supplemental warp chain according to the draft, with 4 background warp threads between supplemental warps and 4 at the end. There should be a total of 32 background warps and 8 supplemental warps in the section. Bundle the section and push aside

Count out 28 background warps for space between supplemental warp sections. Bundle and push to the side.

Thread the second supplemental warp chain as you did the first. When you finish, there should be 24 background warps left to the selvedge.

Step 3 Sley the reed, centering for a 12" weaving width. There will be 1 end/dent in the background-only areas and two threads where a supplemental warp is next to a background warp.

Step 4 Tie on using your preferred method, including the pattern warps with the background warp in the tie-on groups. Weight the supplemental warp bouts over the back beam. Adjust your background warp tension to match that provided by the weights. (Add weight if you like to weave with more tension).

Step 5 Wind a bobbin of weft yarn. Leaving at least 5" for fringe, weave the scarf, moving the weights on the supplemental warp as needed. Figure 2 shows two treadling patterns; switching the treadling moves alternating supplemental warp threads to the top or bottom of the cloth. You could start by weaving 20 inches or so with 8 picks of each treadling before switching, then weave 4 picks of each treadling for a few

Figure 2. Draft

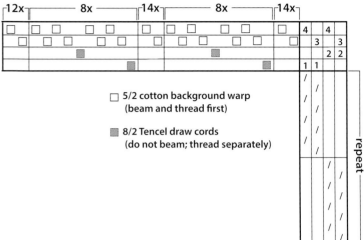

☐ 5/2 cotton background warp (beam and thread first)

▧ 8/2 Tencel draw cords (do not beam; thread separately)

inches, or any other pattern you want. (Don't weave fewer than 4 picks between changes because you do want your cloth to have sizeable gathers when you pull the draw cords.) Try different combinations. Play!

Step 6 Cut the scarf off the loom, allowing 5" for fringe, then tie fringe in overhand knots of 4 background warp threads/knot. Do not tie the supplemental warp threads into the fringe knots! Tie the supplemental warps together with an overhand knot close to the fell line. Be sure to tie knots in both ends of the supplemental warps before going to next step. Tie the supplemental warps for each bundle together with an overhand knot close to the fell line. Be sure to tie knots in both ends of the supplemental warps before going to next step.

Step 7 To gather the cloth for dyeing, pull on one end of the supplemental warps and move the gathers toward the center, then pull on the opposite end of the supplemental warps and move the gathers toward the center. Keep pulling and packing the gathers toward the center until you just can't pack anymore in. (Read the first part of this chapter for detailed instructions.) Tie the supplemental warps in groups of 4 ends with an overhand knot as close as possible to the fell line on each end. Cut off the excess supplemental warp length.

Step 8 Dye the cloth, following the dyeing instructions given earlier in this chapter. Rinse out dye, then lay flat to dry.

Turned Summer and Winter Scarf

Summer and winter is a fun weave structure in its traditional form. Weaving history suggests that the name refers to the "summer" side of the fabric, where the pattern wefts dominate, and "winter" side, where the background dominates the fabric. In traditional summer and winter, the pattern wefts are "tied down" by interlacement with a set of warp threads (usually threaded on shafts 1 and 2) at specific intervals. For design purposes, each block is given a letter designation. Every block uses shafts 1 and 2, plus one more shaft. For example: Block A is threaded 1-3-2-3, repeat. Block B is threaded 1-4-2-4, repeat.

When Block A is treadled, pattern shows in Block A and background in Block B. When Block B is treadled, pattern shows in sections threaded for Block B and background shows in Block A sections. You can weave four blocks of pattern with only six shafts. There is a plain-weave (tabby) weft plus a pattern weft, and weaving requires two shuttles, one for each weft.

The best part of summer and winter is that by changing which of the tie-down shafts are engaged first or in repeating sequences, completely different patterns can be created. It's great fun, but the limitation is that those pattern blocks and any color changes of the pattern wefts must run from selvedge to selvedge.

Turning a summer and winter draft perked in my brain for quite a long time. When the opportunity to create a revised version of this book arose, I decided it was time to test my ideas. The first big question: Do I need to use supplemental warps or could I just wind the pattern wefts at the same time as the background wefts and wind them on the warp beam together? Experimentation began.

It was a short experiment. Yes, you do need supplemental warps for the summer and winter pattern sections. The take-up on the pattern warps is different enough from the tabby (plain weave) background warps that you quickly get into tensioning and tangling issues winding both warps on the same warp beam as one. Trust me on this.

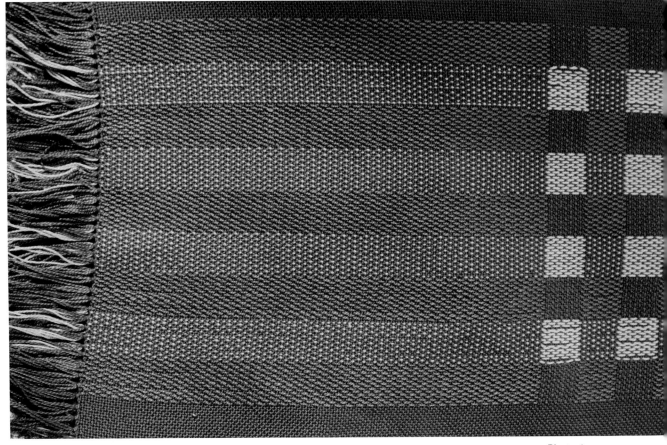

Photo 1

First experiment complete: in a fit of overconfidence, I decided to weave a full-sized table runner without sampling first. I chose 5/2 cotton from Lunatic Fringe for both the background and supplemental pattern warps. Normally, I weave this 5/2 cotton at 16 epi with a firm hand for plain weave, but I worried that the pattern sections would be pretty dense, so I used a sett of 15 epi. This meant using a 10-dent reed sleyed 1-2. I could use a 12-dent reed sleyed 1-1-1-2 for 15 epi, but I was worried about four threads (two background/two supplemental) in the narrower dents of a 12-dent reed. As I wove, occasionally some supplemental warps would squish together in a block. I poked the errant threads back to their correct position, blaming crowded dents, and continued weaving—until about 10 inches into the runner when I suddenly thought, "This is happening on the other side, isn't it?" Yes, it was—I just couldn't see it as clearly on blocks where pattern was on the opposite side. I tweaked, moved, and plucked threads for the rest of the runner. When I took the fabric off the loom, the backside revealed there were many squished-together supplemental warps that I'd missed. To add further insult, after wet-finishing, many of those supplemental warps I'd carefully moved back into place on the top side returned to that squished position. (And no, you can't move them over once the piece is washed. Yes, I tried.) What went wrong? **(See Photos 1 and 2.)**

I became determined to figure this out! More sampling ensued, and I concluded that there were two major issues: (1) tension in the supplemental warp bundles was not consistent across every pattern warp thread in a bundle and (2) changing sides of the fabric with the supplemental wefts wasn't happening cleanly. The threads were catching on the background threads and squishing together, indicating that there wasn't room in the dent for the threads to move cleanly.

I wound a sample of 5/2 to test my conclusions: I (1) divided the supplemental pattern wefts into smaller bundles (half of the threads of each color block in a bundle), (2) I added more weight and wrapped the supplemental warps around the dowel, which ac-

Photo 2

Note: With *traditional* summer and winter, you can weave four blocks of pattern on an 8-shaft loom, using 6 shafts (4 shafts for pattern and 2 shafts for the tabby) and 10 treadles. When *turning* that same 4-block draft, you need 10 shafts: 2 shafts for each block (8 shafts) and 2 more shafts for the plain weave that is engaged with every treadle. A maximum of three blocks of turned summer and winter are possible on an 8-shaft loom with 10 treadles.

tually made the problem worse!, and (3) I spread out the supplemental warps at the back dowel so all the warp threads traveled straight back and didn't twist across each other. This made a *big* difference. Last, (4) I used a reed with larger dents and still obtained correct sett.

Still there were issues. The top layer looked great, and the bottom layer had sporadic sections with squished pattern warps. Now, if I owned a second back beam, I could use it to tension the supplemental warps evenly. If you have one, this is a good weave structure to use it. For those who don't have a second back beam, read on.

Then I had an epiphany (which I seriously credit to Athena whispering in my ear)— what if I left the supplemental warp lease sticks in place when weaving? I never weave with the lease sticks in place because they can cause shed issues if positioned too close to the shafts. But what if I pushed the sticks way back to the back beam, tied the lease stick ends together with a loose figure eight, and draped the weighted supplemental warp bundles over the dowel. It worked! Time for a "real" project.

I warped up a scarf using a scaled-down version of the runner with 8/2 Tencel for the background and a hand-dyed soy silk yarn from my stash for the supplemental warps. The soy silk yarn was marked 10/2 but was about the same grist as the Tencel.

I started weaving, and after 12 inches, I was literally dancing around my studio. All bunched/squished warp problems were gone! It's crucial to (1) have the supplement warp threads travel straight back through the lease sticks to the dowel, (2) pull the supplemental warp bundles taut with each warp advance (yes, you still need to weight each supplemental warp bundle to keep the warp threads taut), and (3) use a quick initial beat on the open shed to pop any stuck supplemental warps into their correct location. On rare occasions, usually after advancing the warp, a supplemental thread would remain caught, but I'd stop, pull a little on the corresponding bundle at the back of the loom, and continued without problems. When I wove the scarf, I only had to tweak individual supplemental bundles 3 or 4 times over the entire length of the weaving, and most importantly, the backside of the fabric was great, too!

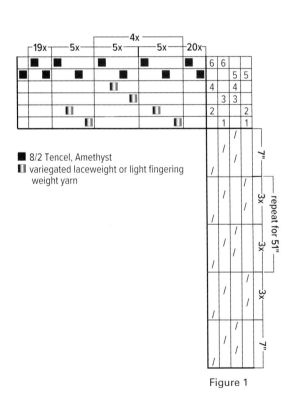

■ 8/2 Tencel, Amethyst
❚ variegated laceweight or light fingering weight yarn

Figure 1

136

Project at a Glance: Turned Summer and Winter Scarf

STRUCTURE
Turned summer and winter

EQUIPMENT
6-shaft loom, 9" weaving width, 10-dent reed, 1 shuttle with bobbin

YARNS
Background warp: 8/2 Tencel (3,360 yd/lb; Valley Yarns; WEBS), Amethyst, 465 yds
Supplemental warps: variegated laceweight or light fingering weight yarn (2,100yd/lb or finer; yarn shown is 10/2 Soy Silk), 293 yds
Weft: 8/2 Tencel, Amethyst, 338 yds

WARP LENGTH
Background warp: 169 warp ends 2¾ yds long (allows 7" for take-up, 27" for loom waste; loom waste includes fringe).
Supplemental Warps: 90 supplemental ends 3¼ yds long (9 bouts, 10 ends per bout).

SETTS
Warp: 20 epi (2 dent in a 10-dent reed). in background-only sections. In supplemental warp sections, sley 2 background and 2 supplemental warp threads per dent.
Weft: 20 ppi

DIMENSIONS
Width in reed: 8 $^5/_{10}$"
Woven length on loom (measured under tension on the loom): 65"
Finished size after washing: 8" x 60" plus fringe

STEP BY STEP INSTRUCTIONS

Step 1 Wind 169 warp ends 2¾ yds long of the background warp. Thread according to directions in Chapter 2, following the draft in Figure 1.

Step 2 Wind supplemental warp of 90 ends 3¼ yds long. In the threading block, there are 9 supplemental warp sections of 10 ends per section. If you want 2 different colors in the supplemental warp sections, wind the color sections individually but next to each other. To make it easy to transfer the warp to the loom: Use a counting thread at the cross to divide the warp into nine sections. Tie choke ties and end ties on *each section*. Place the papers for inserting the lease sticks on each side of the cross so all 90 threads are enclosed by the papers.

Step 3 Lay the supplemental warp on the loom as described in Chapter 2. Insert the lease sticks on each side of the cross. Remove the counting thread at the cross and the papers. Using the choke ties, distribute the sections of supplemental warp across the background warp.

Step 4 Count 40 background warp ends at each selvedge, bundle, and push to the outside edge of the shafts. These will be the plain-weave sections on each side. Thread the supplemental warps, starting after the 40 background warps according to the draft in Figure 1, with 1 background warp thread between each supplemental warp thread.

Step 5 Sley the reed 2 ends/dent in the background-only borders. In the supplemental warp sections, sley two background plus two supplemental warps in each dent. Leave the lease sticks for the supplemental warp in place and push the sticks to the back of the loom. Remove the background warp lease sticks.

Step 6 Tie on, using your preferred method. With this weave structure, I found it works best to tie on the background warps first to the apron rod and then tie on the supplemental warps, using the shoelace method in Chapter 2. Weight the supplemental warp sections, pulling each section taut.

Step 7 Wind a bobbin with weft yarn. Weave 6" of waste yarn for fringe, checking for any tensioning issues. Weave the scarf according to the draft, Figure 1: 7" of block A, then alternate weaving block A and block B (12 picks each block, about 5/8") until the scarf measures 58", finishing with 7" of block A.

Step 8 Remove scarf from the loom, leaving at least 8" of warp for fringe. Remove the waste yarn and tie overhand knots against the ends of the scarf in warp.

Step 9 Handwash in warm water and lay flat to dry. Tencel will feel stiff after washing. Don't worry; it will soften up nicely once dry.

Step 10 Trim fringes to desired length. Strut your stuff!

Appendix

Now that you're ready to begin your own adventures in weaving with supplemental warp, here are a few more words of advice, and some resources to help make your weaving life easier.

ON THE BENEFITS OF RECORD KEEPING

Once upon a time, I had a very wise weaving teacher who told us to keep records of all of our projects. She told us that even though we think we will always remember why, when, and how we wove something, it won't happen. At minimum, she said, your records should include a picture of the project, a copy of the draft, and all notes on warp calculations, yarn used, and why you wove it the way you did. Keep all those records in one place.

I listened—sort of—and kept a spiral notebook. I stapled a copy of the draft to a page, taped samples of the yarn I used, and recorded calculations. That system soon devolved into "stuff the picture and draft into the notebook, and I'll do a better job later, when I have time." Well (and you know the next part of this story), "later" still hasn't arrived, and that notebook is still stuffed with information that has no rhyme or reason.

People tend to fall into two camps for organizing records—"filers" and "pilers." Filers put things in their place, and they regularly sort out unnecessary items and toss them, sooner rather than later. My husband is a filer. Then there are pilers. Pilers have a place for everything; it's just in piles. And things in the piles may be related, or not. Eventually pilers go through the piles and sort things out. Don't get me wrong; pilers know which pile something is in, and where in the pile. Their "system" is just a little slower and messier. Creative people tend to be pilers (I swear! Yes, it's been studied!). I'm a piler, and it makes my husband crazy.

In 2002, I decided to work toward the Handweaver's Guild of America (HGA) Certificate of Excellence, Level 1 in handweaving. Record keeping is a very large and serious part of the Certificate of Excellence program. Thankfully, the independent study workbook included a very good record-keeping worksheet. I became much more disciplined in my record keeping, and it's a habit I have kept.

Over the years, I've adapted the HGA record-keeping sheet to include all the information I like to use. I have a three-ring binder that has dividers marked for scarves, runners, shawls, etc., so that when I look for a project, I'm not flipping through years of different projects. Each project has a record sheet, samples of the yarns used in the project (and all my cones now have a sticker inside the cone, listing the source and fiber content), a copy of the full drawdown draft, any notes and observations I made while weaving, and a picture of the finished project (OK, I admit, there's not always a picture). I give myself bonus points if I included a woven sample. If I'm selling the finished project, I keep a studio log where I record the time spent on it, from design through finishing. I still have to resist the urge to just stuff all the sheets into the notebook, but the two minutes it takes to punch holes in the papers and put the record sheets in the binder is time well spent.

I'm including the record-keeping sheet that I use. As I researched this book, I realized how much we modern handweavers owe to the generations before us who wrote down their drafts and other weaving information. Their efforts helped handweaving survive the advent of mechanized looms. Who knows, maybe someday in the future, your records will be treasured by another weaver or a guilld. And they won't have to sort through your piles!

Note: Formulas for calculating sett and warp amounts can be found in Chapter 4. The formula for calculating pile warp amounts can be found in Project 6, the terry cloth towels.

RECORDS WORKSHEET

Pattern Name _____

Warp length _____

(_____ (woven length) + _____(takeup) + _____ fringe + _____ Loom waste)

Warp Yarn: _____   Price per oz: _____

Sett: _____   Wound Warp Weight: _____

Warp Cost: _____

Total number of warp threads: _____

(floating selvedges?   Yes   No)

# of warp Bundles: _____   _____

Tabby Weft Yarn (supplier/name): _____

Tabby Weft Yarn Color: _____   Price per oz: _____

Tabby Weft Yardage: _____   Tabby Weft Weight: _____

Tabby Weft Cost: _____

Pattern Weft Yarn (supplier/name): _____

Pattern Weft Yarn Color: _____   Price per oz: _____

Pattern Weft Yardage: _____   Pattern Weft Weight: _____

Pattern Weft Cost: _____

Weaving (special notes on back):

Hem/header: _____

Fringe Finish: _____

Floating Selvedge weaving order: From right: _____

                                     From Left: _____

Width in Reed: _____   Woven Length on loom: _____

Length off loom (unwashed): _____   Width off loom (unwashed): _____

Finished length (washed): _____   Finished width (washed): _____

Resources

WEAVING BOOKS

A Handweaver's Pattern Book by Marguerite Porter Davison. Swarthmore, Pennsylvania: Marguerite P. Davison, 1944. "Monk's Belt (Traditional Drafts)," pp. 101–108.

Interweave's Compendium of Finishing Techniques by Naomi McEneely, ed. Loveland, Colorado: Interweave, 2003. Twisted fringe, p. 33; knotted fringe, p. 41.

Mastering Weave Structures: Transforming Ideas into Great Cloth by Sharon Alderman. Loveland, Colorado: Interweave, 2004. "Bedford Cord and Piqués," pp. 179–188.

Velvet on My Mind by Wendy Landry. Atglen, PA: Schiffer Publishing, 2020. In depth information on weaving velvet and additional velvet weaving techniques for handweavers.

Weaving Overshot: Redesigning the Tradition by Donna Lee Sullivan. Loveland, Colorado: Interweave, 1996.

Woven Shibori by Catharine Ellis. Loveland, Colorado: Interweave, 2016. "Supplemental Warps," pp. 63–69; "Dyes and Special Effects," pp. 85–103; "Dye Recipes," pp. 106–117.

DYEING BOOKS

Color in Spinning by Deb Menz. Loveland, Colorado: Interweave, 2005.

Colors from Nature by Bobbi A McRae. Pownal, Vermont: Storey, 1993.

Hands On Dyeing by Betsy Blumenthal and Kathryn Kreider. Loveland, Colorado: Interweave, 1988.

The Surface Designer's Handbook by Holly Brackmann. Loveland, Colorado: Interweave, 2006.

OTHER USEFUL BOOKS

In Sheep's Clothing: A Handspinner's Guide to Wool by Nola Fournier and Jane Fournier. Loveland, Colorado: Interweave, 1995. Bradford count and micron measurements, p. 18.

The Knitter's Companion by Vicki Square. Loveland, Colorado: Interweave, 2006.

The Practical Spinner's Guide: Cotton, Flax, Hemp by Stephenie Gaustad. Loveland, Colorado: Interweave, 2014. Linen spinning, weaving, and finishing, pp. 53–93.

Women's Work: The First 20,000 Years: Women, Cloth, and Society in Early Times by Elizabeth Wayland Barber. New York: Norton, 1994. Athena stories in Greek mythology.

MAGAZINE ARTICLES

"Small-scale velvet for an evening bag," by Robin Spady. *Handwoven* January/February 2010, p. 44–46.

"Sumptuous terry cloth: take it for a spin," by Rita Buchanan. *Handwoven*, November/December 2010, p. 46–49.

"Turned Drafts," by Kathryn Wertenberger. *Handwoven*, May/June 1985, p. 90–94.

ON THE WEB

"Adventures in Velvet Weaving," by Suzi Gough. *Journal for Weavers, Spinners and Dyers*, March 2007. www.the journalforwsd.org.uk/application/workfiles/resources/art221.pdf.

"Fashion Fabrics—Velvet in Fashion, 2005–2006" by Pauline Weston Thomas for Fashion-Era.com. www.fashion-era.com/velvets/velvet.htm.

"Figured Velvets from Simple Looms: Velvet Pick-Up and Related Techniques for Handweavers" by Wendy Landry. 2010 Textile Society of America Symposium. DigitalCommons@University of Nebraska-Lincoln. www.digitalcommons.unl.edu.

"Terry Weaving." textlnfo.files.wordpress.com/2011/10/terry-towel.pdf.

"The Encyclopedia of the Goddess Athena," story adapted from *Bulfinch's Mythology: The Age of Fable*, Chapter XIV, Minerva Niobe. www.goddess-athena.org/Encyclopedia/Athena/Arachne.htm.

"Velvet." http://en.wikipedia.org/wiki/Velvet.

YARN SUPPLIERS

Glimakra USA: Bockens Linen and cotton yarns. glimakrausa.com.

Jagger Spun Yarns: Zephyr wool/silk blend, www.jaggeryarn.com and other yarn retailers

Lunatic Fringe Yarns: Tubular Spectrum mercerized cotton. https://lunaticfringeyarns.com

Mountain Colors Yarns: hand-painted knitting yarns, www.mountaincolors.com and yarn retailers

New World Textiles: Dye-lishus cotton in 5/2, 5/4, and 10/2. www.newworldtextiles.com.

Webs: Pearl cotton in 3/2, 5/2, and 10/2; 8/2 Tencel and bamboo. www.yarn.com.

About the author

Deb Essen watched a weaver perform "magic" on a loom for the first time at just nine years old. Enticed by that memory, she finally took her first weaving class in 1993, and she's been exploring weaving ever since. She lives, weaves, and runs her business, DJE Handwovens, in the Bitterroot Valley, nestled in the Rocky Mountains of western Montana. In 2004, Deb achieved the Certificate of Excellence in Handweaving Level 1 through the Handweaver's Guild of America and, in 2011, was recognized by the Montana Arts Council with an induction into the Montana Circle of American Masters in Folk and Traditional Art. She has written multiple feature articles for *Handwoven* and *Little Looms* magazines. Deb is passionate about teaching about the wonders of weaving and shares her knowledge at shops, guilds, and regional and national conferences and festivals.
www.djehandwovens.com

Acknowledgments

I always say that life is deciding which fork in the road should be taken at certain times. This book was originally published in 2016 by Interweave Press, a division of F + W Media. In 2019, F + W Media reorganized and sold off several parts of the business, including the book division. The book division was purchased by Penguin Random House, and I found out in 2020 (just as the COVID-19 pandemic was gathering steam) that the e-book file was missing in action from the sale and PRH didn't intend to reprint the book. At that point, I requested the legal rights to the book be returned to me. Fast-forward to late 2020: Schiffer Publishing accepted the book for publication, and I commenced on the revised version.

Getting a book out into the world is not a solitary endeavor. Many individuals work "behind the scenes" to make this publication possible, and I thank everyone involved from the bottom of my heart.

But there are a special few I need to acknowledge individually, because without them, you wouldn't be reading this book.

First and foremost, my husband, Marty Essen, who is not only my biggest cheerleader and sounding board but also the photographer for almost all of the pictures in this book. In so many ways, I couldn't have done this without him.

Anita Osterhaug, who was the editor, author guide, and advocate for the original book published by Interweave Press. She is the mastermind behind replacing the formal studio project shots with photos staged in Montana's landscape and photographed by Marty. I admit, at the time, this idea gave me a little heartburn. But she was spot on.

Sandra Kornichak at Schiffer Publishing for believing in reissuing the book and guiding it (and me) through the process.